MAY 17 1922

Republic of Costa Rica.

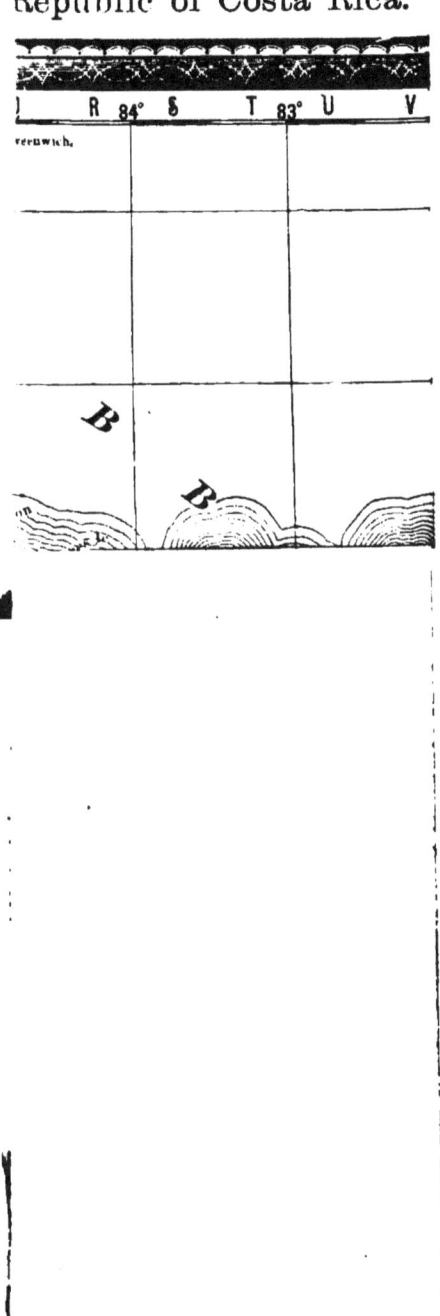

R 84° S   T 83° U   V

reenwich.

Don Bernardo Soto, President of Costa Rica.

THE REPUBLIC

OF

COSTA RICA

BY

JOAQUIN BERNARDO CALVO.

TRANSLATED FROM THE SPANISH AND
EDITED BY

L. de T.

WITH INTRODUCTION, ADDITIONS, AND EXTENSIONS BY

THE EDITOR.

MAP AND ILLUSTRATIONS.

CHICAGO AND NEW YORK:
RAND, McNALLY & COMPANY, PUBLISHERS.
1890.

COPYRIGHT 1889, BY RAND, MCNALLY & CO.

Costa Rica.

AUTHOR'S DEDICATION.

To the Señor Licenciado Don Bernardo Soto,
President of the Republic,
in testimony of friendship and gratitude for
assistance accorded in the publication of this work;

To the Señores Don Leon Fernandez and
Don Manuel María Peralta,
as a tribute of admiration for their industry
and patriotism as demonstrated in their
works in connection with the
national history;

AND

To the Señores Don Francisco María Iglesias,
Doctor Don Rafael Machado, and
Don Miguel Obregón L.,
for their abnegation and disinterestedness in the
discharge of official duty in judging of this
effort, and for the kindly sentiments of their report,
this book is dedicated by
the author.

To
THE PEOPLE OF COSTA RICA.
WITH
THE AFFECTIONATE ESTEEM
OF
THE EDITOR.

CONTENTS.

PART I.

	PAGE.
Agricultural Statistics	67
Alajuela	203
Animal Kingdom	70
Aquatic Birds	113
Arms and Colors	40
Army	178
Atenas	150
Bananas	65
Banking Houses	140
Birds	81
Boundaries	20
Cable	158
Cartago	198
Census	50
Climate	48
Cocoa—Chocolate	63
Cocoanuts	62
Coffee	65
Coffee Product 1888	138
Coffee Export 1888	136
Commerce	131
Corn	63
Cotton	62
Distinguished Men	182
Esparta	149
Extent of Territory	19
Factories	129
Fine Arts	180

CONTENTS.

	PAGE.
Fish, Mollusks, Crustaceans, etc.	118
Foreigners	52
Foreign Debt	175
Fruits	63
Garita	150
Geographical Position	19
Grape-vine	62
Gulfs and Bays	44
Heredia	205
Importations	138
Indigo	63
Industries and Arts	119
Instruction	165
Interior Debt	177
International Relations	178
Inter-oceanic Road	148
Islands	47
Lakes	45
Legislation and Courts	170
Liberia	206
Limon	152
Live-stock Industry	120
Mails	155
Mammalia	71
Manufactories	126
Medicinal and Oleaginous Plants	58
Mineral Kingdom	68
Mining Industry	122
Miscellaneous Societies	140
Moneys	141
National Bills	177
National Debt	175
National Income	174
National Products	67
National Revenues	172
Newspapers	179
Nicoya	206
Occupations	53

CONTENTS.

	PAGE.
Origin of Name	39
Peninsulas and Capes	45
Physiognomy of Country	42
Political Institutions	159
Population and Character	49–51
Potatoes	63
Principal Towns	187
Printing	179
Productions	54
Provinces and Districts	167
Public Administration	160
Punishments	172
Puntarenas	148
Registration of Property	172
Religion	161
Reptiles and Batrachia	115
Rice	63
Rights and Privileges	161
Rivers	46
Rubber	61
San José	187
San Mateo	149
Santa Cruz	206
Sarsaparilla	62
Seasons	49
School Districts	167
Sugar-cane	64
Telegraph and Telephone	158–159
Textile Plants and Dye Plants	59
Tobacco	63
Value of Foreign Moneys	144
Vegetable Kingdom	55
Volcanoes	44
Ways of Communication	147
Weights and Measures	144
Wheat	64
Wood	60
Workshops	128

CONTENTS.

PART II.

	PAGE.
First Period—Spanish Rule	209
Founding of Talamanca, its Destruction, etc.—1605 to 1665	221
Decay of the Province—1666 to 1727	224
Eruption of Irazu—1723	229
Improvement and Reanimation—1727 to 1821	231
Governors of Costa Rica under the Spanish Rule	236
Second Period—Independence of Costa Rica—1811 to 1825	237
Events in Costa Rica	241
Declaration of Independence	244
First Constitutive Law and Annexation to Mexico	248
First Civil War	251
First Congress or Constituent Assembly	261
Presidents from 1824	264

PART III.

How to Go to Costa Rica	267
What to Wear	271
Money	272
How to Live, and Where	272
Don Juan Mora	274
Don José Rafael Gallegos	275
Don Manuel Aguilar	276
Don Braulio Carrillo	277
General Don Francisco Morazan	278
Don José Maria Alfaro	279
Don Francisco Maria Oreamuno	280
Doctor Don José Maria Castro	280
Don Juan Rafael Mora	281
Don José Maria Montealegre	282
Don Jesus Jiménez	283
General Don Tomas Guardia	284
General Don Prospero Fernandez	285
President Soto	285
Licentiate Don Ascension Esquivel	286
The Costa Rica Railway	286

EDITOR'S INTRODUCTION.

The task of translating any work, however interesting the original, must always be found more or less tedious. Just when the pen would run on most steadily, and when the brain is most absorbed with the subject, one is apt to arrive at some expression, the rendering of which into another and perhaps less graceful language, without reducing it to bald ugliness, is so difficult as to tempt one to forego it.

Señor Calvo's book is, however, a work so rich in information, so admirably compact, and withal so well adapted to supply practical knowledge, that I have found little to abridge or dispense with. It is a book for all who would know something of Costa Rica; for the capitalist or speculator interested in mining, manufacturing, or agricultural enterprises; for the less fortunate who seek to build themselves up fortunes remote from the pitiless pressure and selfishness of great Northern cities; for the traveler who would view new sights; the pleasure seeker tired of beaten tracks; the sportsman wishing to surprise himself and his friends, and for the invalid whose days are shadowed by merciless disease.

I am not overenthusiastic nor disposed to exaggerate, I believe, when I assert, that if one-fiftieth part of the inhabitants of the North had the faintest approach to a true idea of the Republic of Costa Rica, its superb mountains, its inexpressible loveliness of valleys, its atmosphere of eternal May, its remarkable advancement in ways of civilization, its cultured, courteous, hospitable people, not all the hotels in San José could begin to accommodate the eager crowds that would pour down by every steamer.

In this belief I have sought to render the best and most authentic information accessible to the people of the United States, the greater part of whom are, at present, so phenomenally and deplorably ignorant of the superb countries lying south of the blue Caribbean.

L. DE T.

SAN JOSÉ, Feb. 1, 1889.

PRESENTATION OF ORIGINAL WORK TO THE GOVERNMENT AND DECREE OF THE MINISTER OF PUBLIC WORKS.

To the Minister of Public Works:

Sir:—I have compiled and arranged a series of "Notes—Geographical, Statistical, and Historical—of the Republic of Costa Rica," endeavoring, as far as possible, to observe the truth and accuracy required in a work of this nature. The task has been arduous; but, undertaken with a resolute spirit, in the desire of being of service to my country, I have not faltered in carrying it out, believing that it may possess some interest, even although the works of persons of greater ability may soon appear.

In order to give authenticity to my modest work, should it merit attention, I consider it indispensable that a Commission, officially appointed, should examine it, and render an impartial verdict; in behalf of which, I have come, Sir, asking that you will be pleased to appoint such Commission, and hoping that those composing it may not find their task distasteful.

I place in your hands my work, and with the hope of a just decision of the Ministry upon its merits, I have the honor to subscribe myself,

Your obedient and faithful servant,

J. B. CALVO.

San José, Nov. 23, 1886.

[No. 113.]

THE NATIONAL PALACE,
SAN JOSÉ, Nov. 24, 1886.

Having taken under consideration the memorial in which Don Joaquin Bernardo Calvo petitions for the appointment of a Commission to examine the work which he has written, with the title, "Notes—Geographical, Statistical, and Historical—of the Republic of Costa Rica," and to report to this secretaryship upon its merits, the Vice-President, in exercise of the Presidency of the Republic,

DECREES:

To accede to the petition, and to intrust the task of examination and reporting upon the work in question to Doctor Don Rafael Machado, Don Francisco Maria Iglesias, and Don Miguel Obregon.

[Signed and sealed by the Vice-President in exercise of the Presidency of the Republic.]

LIZANO.

REPORT OF THE COMMISSION AND DECREE OF THE MINISTER OF PUBLIC INSTRUCTION.

To the Secretary of State in the Office of Public Works:

Sir:—We have read and examined carefully the manuscripts of Don Joaquin Bernardo Calvo, entitled, "Notes—Geographical, Statistical, and Historical—of the Republic of Costa Rica," fulfilling thus the honorable duty with which we were intrusted by decree of the 24th of November last.

The labors of Mr. Calvo are worthy of all praise, being proof-patent of his intelligence and industry.

It is time that a work of this nature should be written by a son of Costa Rica, to fill the want which has existed for so many years, of a compilation of facts, geographical, statistical, and historical, about the country.

Until now the "Bosquejo Historico" of the never-to-be-forgotten Central American, son by adoption of Costa Rica, Don Felipe Molina, has been the only work of the kind published; further, by reason of the time in which it was written, and the want of that information, geographical, statistical, and historical, which has since been obtained, it was lacking in much for which it might be consulted, and was not satisfactory in the advance and progress of the present epoch.

Although in later years some treatises have appeared in Spanish, these are so rudimentary that their usefulness can not go beyond the elementary schools, or certain mercantile circles, to which it is necessary to transmit incompletely and briefly the most indispensable points about our little-known country.

Mr. Calvo's work will replace, with a thousand advantages, that of Mr. Molina, and chiefly will it prove invaluable to the foreigner. The geographical and statistical information is taken from the most recent letters and official publications; as for the historical facts, they flow from the best sources, from authentic documents.

Works of this kind stimulate the study and investigation of facts, and give origin to works still more extensive and complete, preparing the way so that one day there may be written upon the same useful, interesting, and extensive subjects a work truly classic and actually national.

Without entering into details as to the plan, division, and merits of Mr. Calvo's book, we are pleased to recommend it to the especial protection of the Government, and we predict, upon its publication, success and a favorable reception in this and other countries.

We are, with all consideration, your obedient and faithful servants,

FRANCISCO M. IGLESIAS.
RAFAEL MACHADO.
MIGUEL OBREGON L.

[No. 178.]

THE NATIONAL PALACE,
SAN JOSÉ, Dec. 20, 1886.

Having taken under consideration the petition of Don Joaquin Bernardo Calvo, in which he asks that the " Notes—Geographical. Statistical, and Historical—of the Republic of Costa Rica," which he has compiled and arranged, be declared his absolute property, and that he be aided in its publication by the printing of it at public expense; and having seen the favorable report made upon this work by the Commission appointed for that purpose, and the publication being of national interest, the General President of the Republic

DECREES:

To declare the absolute property of Mr. Calvo the work entitled, "Notes—Geographical, Statistical, and Historical—of the Republic of Costa Rica;" and that out of the appropriation for Public Instruction, the printing of three thousand copies shall be paid for, of which the Government shall reserve five hundred. Be it communicated.

[Signed and sealed by the President of the Republic.]

FERNANDEZ.

Don Tomas Guardia

THE REPUBLIC OF COSTA RICA.

PART I.

GEOGRAPHICAL POSITION.

Central America comprises the five Republics Guatemala, Salvador, Honduras, Nicaragua, and Costa Rica, which, together with the State of Chiapas and Soconusco, to-day of the Mexican Republic, formed the ancient Kingdom of Guatemala under the Spanish Colonial Government, whose territory, after the Proclamation of Independence, the 15th of September, 1821, constituted the Federal Republic of Central America, dissolved in the year 1840.

The Republic of Costa Rica is situated in the southeastern extremity of Central America, between 8° and 11° 16' North Latitude, and 81° 40' and 85° 40' West Longitude from Greenwich.

EXTENT OF TERRITORY.

The territory of the Republic embraces an area calculated at 59,570 square kilometers (31,220½ square miles), a little less than the area of West Virginia, and about double that of Switzerland, bounded by the following

LIMITS.

On the north and east, the Republic of Nicaragua and the Atlantic Ocean; on the south and west, the Pacific Ocean and the State of Panama, of the Republic of Colombia.

The earliest boundaries of Costa Rica were marked, on the north, from the mouth of the River San Juan to the Island Escudo de Veraguas; and on the south, from the River Salto, or Alvarado, to the mouth of the River Chiriqui Viejo. The district of Nicoya, to-day Province of Guanacaste, constituted an Alcaldia, which was suppressed in 1750, and the district made subject to the Governor of Costa Rica, by virtue of royal command; later a new order was established, and a sub-Delegate appointed Administrator of the district. For the election of Representatives to the Assembly of the Realm, according to the Constitution of 1812, it again joined itself to Costa Rica, and so remained from then on.

After the Independence, and in the shelter of a peace almost uninterrupted, Costa Rica established herself, and tranquilly followed her march of progress, while in Nicaragua discord was hatched and civil war enkindled.

The inhabitants of Guanacaste regarded and compared the condition of the two countries, and with a spontaneous movement petitioned, in 1824, for definite incorporation with Costa Rica.

This State accepted the annexation in 1825, and the first Federal Congress of Central America, which succeeded the Constitutional Assembly, approved it by decree on the 9th of December of the same year, reserving until later the demarkation of territory of each of the States.

There were present at this Congress representatives of Nicaragua; but disapproval was manifested in that State, and many attempts were made to reclaim Guanacaste.

In 1838, Nicaragua desiring to fix the boundary line at the River Salto, the Costarican Government, through its Minister Plenipotentiary, Don Francisco Maria Oreamuno, asked that the annexation of Guanacaste to this State be recognized as perpetual, and declared its resolve to maintain the boundary line at the River San Juan, the Great Lake, and the River La Flor, leaving unsettled the claims of the other State.

The final attempt of General Don Francisco Morazan, in Costa Rica, in 1842, to reorganize Central America, produced alarm in the other States, and these prepared for war. Nicaragua believed the circumstances favorable to its designs upon Guanacaste, and the 4th of June of the same year the Congress of that State issued a decree advising the Executive Power that it should proceed to recover the Department in question.

The government of General Morazan being overthrown by insurrection of the people, the new administration was not yet firm when Nicaragua, through its Envoy, the Licenciado Don Toribio Tijerino, demanded the restitution of the disputed territory; but the Government of Costa Rica, which it had believed weak, protested against the demand, and the condition of affairs remained unchanged.

Later, after a ministerial correspondence between the two Cabinets, the Costarican Government proposed that if the reunion of the Federal Congress was rendered difficult, the question be submitted to an arbitration of one or more Central American States; and Nicaragua "believed it should refuse to agree to this proposition, for the reason that the other States were not in a position to inspire the required confidence."

In 1846, it being considered that the better way for the commerce of the country to direct itself was to the San Juan, by one of its tributaries, the Government of Costa Rica sent to Nicaragua Don Juan Vicente Escalante and the Rev. Dr. Don Juan de los Santos Madriz, in order to come to an agreement with the Government of the other State, which at that time occupied the port of San Juan.

Nicaragua, notwithstanding the indisputable right of Costa Rica to that way of communication, "responded in terms which demonstrated at once ignorance of her own interests and a disposition far from friendly toward Costa Rica."

Under such circumstances, the Costarican Envoy could obtain no favorable solution; the Governments of Guatemala and Honduras were named to arbitrate in reference to Guanacaste, but this was not acceptable to Costa Rica, who would in nowise consent to place in doubt her rights to the said territory.

A new attempt to settle the question was put in operation in 1848. The Government of Costa Rica, desiring to open a route by the River Sarapiqui and the San Juan toward the Atlantic, sought to come to an agreement with that of Nicaragua, and for the purpose named as its representative Don Felipe Molina. The result of the conference reduced itself to an absurd demand from Nicaragua that Costa Rica give up either Guanacaste or the Sarapiqui and San Juan.

An attempt was then made to submit the question to Guatemala, Nicaragua not having accepted the other neighbor-countries; but the adjustments proposed by Mr. Molina were never completed. "The Nicaraguan Minister, Juarez, signed an agreement one day, and the next withdrew his signature, saying that his Government had not approved of it." The secret of these vacillations and contrarieties was the confidence felt by Nicaragua that its Minister in London would conclude satisfactorily the negotiations begun for the building of the canal.

The injustice of Nicaragua in attempting to deny Costa Rica's unquestionable rights to the River San Juan, in order to deprive her of any share in the desired canal, was the reason why no agreement could be reached, until the war with the "Filibusters" passed, the other governments of Central America bringing weighty influence to bear toward the settlement of the question with the "Cañas-Jerez" treaty of 1858.

Costa Rica, in deference to the tranquillity of Central America, ceded many of her rights, but always caused to be recognized that over the River San Juan.

Article 2 of the treaty says:

"The dividing line, starting from the Atlantic, shall begin at the extremity of Punta de Castilla, at the mouth of the San Juan River, and shall continue following the right bank of that river to a point situated in the water below the castle, and three miles from the fortifications. From that point there shall go a curve, whose center shall be the same fortifications, and said curve shall be always three miles distant, as far as the other point in the water above the castle, and two miles from the bank of the river. From that point on, the dividing line shall continue parallel to the turns of the river and to the southern shore of the lake, always two miles distant, until it shall reach the River Sapoa. From the point where it shall meet the Sapoa, a point well understood to be two miles from the lake, shall be traced an astronomical line as far as the center of the Bay of Salinas, in the Pacific, where shall terminate the dividing line of the two republics here stipulating."

The treaty was completed with all the customary formalities, exchanged, published, made known by both sides to foreign governments, and observed as a law between the two countries, until fifteen years afterward the Nicaraguan Government sought to place in doubt its validity, supporting itself with arguments that Costa Rica could not recognize as sound, notwithstanding that in case of the document being declared invalid she would recover her limits as far as La Flor, the Gran Lago, and the River San Juan.

The justness of Costa Rica has been so clear, and her course so honest, that eminent Nicaraguans have proclaimed as much in the very capital of that country.

In October, 1873, the Nicaraguan Senate discussed the treaty of alliance between Nicaragua, Salvador, and Guatemala. In the heat of debate upon this subject was heard the authoritative voice of an immortal patriot, General Don Maximo Jerez. What soundness of judgment! What nobility of sentiment! How simple, and yet how lofty, his eloquence!

General Jerez perceived in the treaty of alliance a violation of Articles 2 and 3 of the friendly treaty between Nicaragua and Costa Rica, which agree that neither of the two republics shall make war against the other, or enter into offensive alliances, without previously having asked explanations or demanded the same, and without having exhausted all means for arriving at a peaceable settlement.

General Jerez perceived in the treaty of alliance a declaration of war against Costa Rica, sent forth without observance of the treaty, and, in any case, the gravest violation of the Constitution of Nicaragua. He did not undertake to point out that the approval of such a compact signified a declaration of war, for no one denied this, but he showed that in case any objections were offered, an unavoidable dilemma occurred. By approval of the treaty, he said, war was decreed or not decreed. If the first, international rights and former treaties were violated; if the second, in addition to these violations there was an infringement of the Constitution of the Republic, since the Government, and, what was worse, the majority of the other governments, were empowered to decree war.

We need not analyze minutely the magnificent speech of General Jerez on this occasion, but we may, at least, copy the text of his discourse concerning the question of limits, because, proceeding from the famous Nicaraguan, they are of far greater value than aught we might say upon the subject:

"*From the beginning of this question as to the validity or invalidity of the 1858 treaty of limits, I have always thought that we had the worst of it. It has always seemed to me that to concede the reasons now quoted as opposing the understanding we had of the Nicaraguan laws at the time of the treaty, would reflect seriously upon that understanding; and never, in any case, would I deem it fitting that the Nicaraguan authorities, in order to annul the said treaty, should declare, in the face of all the world, that, being children, they had not comprehended, nor were they obliged to comprehend, the meaning of their own laws.*

"*Perhaps it is for sentiments similar to those I have just expressed, that Congress has been silent upon this unfortunate question, submitted to it some time since for consideration by the Government, of the invalidity of the treaty referred to, notwithstanding it is seen that this treaty, exchanged in 1858, and executed in good faith fifteen years since, continues to be observed."*

Another illustrious son of Nicaragua, in the editorial column of an important Guatemala newspaper, says as follows:

"In Nicaragua it is known, even down to babes in arms, that the Liberian folk are, in education, sympathy, and customs, essentially Costarican, and we do not believe it wise that Nicaragua should indulge in the whim of giving a people to a country to which they do not incline, with injury to the general peace of the State."

These words comprehended another strong argument concerning Guanacaste.

In respect to the River San Juan, under the new aspect of the invalidity of the treaty of 1858, the Nicaraguan Government dismissed the question, treating it even in such a way as to attempt to deny this Republic the free use of the waters of the river, notwithstanding the indisputable early rights of Costa Rica, and the agreement of Article 6 of the treaty.

The Government of Guatemala having offered its friendly mediation, an effort was made before it for the final solution of the question.

Still later, the question was submitted for arbitration to the President of the United States, by virtue of a treaty signed at the City of Guatemala, on the 24th day of December, 1886, between the contracting governments.

By this treaty it was agreed that, if the arbitrator's award should determine that the treaty of the 15th day of April, 1858, was valid, the same award should also declare whether Costa Rica has the right of navigation of the River San Juan, with vessels of war or of the revenue service, and other points. The decision of President Cleveland, given on the 22d of March, 1888, is as follows:

"1st. The above-mentioned treaty of limits, signed on the 15th day of April, 1858, is valid.

"2d. The Republic of Costa Rica, under said treaty, and the stipulations contained in the 6th article thereof, has not the right of navigation of the River San Juan with vessels of war, but she may navigate said river with such vessels of revenue service as may be related to and connected with her enjoyment of the 'purposes of commerce' accorded to her in said articles, or as may be necessary to the protection of said enjoyments."

"1. The boundary line between the Republics of Costa Rica and Nicaragua, on the Atlantic side, begins at the extremity of Punta de Castilla, at the mouth of the San Juan de Nicaragua River, as they both existed on the 15th day of April, 1858. The ownership of any accretion to said Punta de Castilla is to be governed by the laws applicable to that subject.

"2. The central point of the Salinas Bay is to be fixed by drawing a straight line across the mouth of the bay, and determining mathematically the center of the closed geometrical figure formed by such straight line and the shore of the bay at low-water mark.

"3. By the central point of Salinas Bay is to be understood the center of the geometrical figure formed as above stated. The limit of the bay toward the ocean is a straight line drawn from the extremity of Punta Arranca Barba, nearly true south to the westernmost portion of the land about Punta Sacate.

"4. The Republic of Costa Rica is not bound to concur with the Republic of Nicaragua in the expenses necessary to prevent the Bay of San Juan del Norte from being obstructed; to keep the navigation of the river or port free and unembarrassed, or to improve it for the common benefit.

"5. The Republic of Costa Rica is not bound to contribute any portion of the expenses that may be incurred by the Republic of Nicaragua for any of the purposes above mentioned.

"6. The Republic of Costa Rica can not prevent the Republic of Nicaragua from executing at her own expense and within her own territory any works of improvement, *provided* such works of improvement do not result in the occupation or flooding or damage of Costarican territory, or in the destruction or serious impairment of the navigation of the said river, or any of its branches, at any point where Costa

Rica is entitled to navigate the same. The Republic of Costa Rica has the right to demand indemnification for any places belonging to her on the right bank of the River San Juan which may be occupied without her consent, and for any lands on the same bank which may be flooded, or damaged in any other way, in consequence of said works of improvement.

"7. The branch of the River San Juan known as the Colorado River must not be considered as the boundary between the Republics of Costa Rica and Nicaragua in any part of its course.

"8. The right of the Republic of Costa Rica to the navigation of the River San Juan with men-of-war or revenue cutters is determined and defined in the second article of this award.

"9. The Republic of Costa Rica can deny to the Republic of Nicaragua the right of deviating the waters of the River San Juan, in case such deviation will result in the destruction or serious impairment of the navigation of the said river, or any of its branches, at any point where Costa Rica is entitled to navigate the same.

"10. The Republic of Nicaragua remains bound not to make any grants for canal purposes across her territory without first asking the opinion of the Republic of Costa Rica, as provided in Article 8 of the Treaty of Limits of the 15th of April, 1858. The natural rights of the Republic of Costa Rica, alluded to in the said stipulation, are the rights which, in view of the boundaries fixed by the said Treaty of Limits, she possesses in the soil thereby recognized as belonging exclusively to her; the rights which she possesses in the harbors of San Juan del Norte and Salinas Bay; and the rights which she possesses in so much of the River San Juan as lies more than three English miles below Castillo Viejo, measuring from the exterior fortifications of the said castle as the same existed in the year 1858; and perhaps other rights not here particularly specified. These rights are to be deemed injured in any case where the territory, belonging to the Republic of Costa Rica, is occupied or flooded; where there is an encroachment upon either of the said harbors injurious to Costa Rica, or where there is such an obstruction or deviation of the River San Juan as to destroy or seriously impair the navigation of the said river or any of its branches at any point where Costa Rica is entitled to navigate the same.

"11. The Treaty of Limits of the 15th day of April, 1858, does not give to the Republic of Costa Rica the right to be a party to grants which Nicaragua may make for inter-oceanic canals; though in cases where the construction of the canal will involve an injury to the natural rights of Costa Rica, her opinion or advice, as mentioned in Article 8 of the

Treaty, should be more than 'advisory' or 'consultative.' It would seem in such cases that her consent is necessary, and that she may thereupon demand compensation for the concessions she is asked to make; but she is not entitled as a right to share in the profits that the Republic of Nicaragua may reserve for herself as a compensation for such favors and privileges as she in her turn may concede."

On the Colombia side, as has been already said, the historical limits of Costa Rica were placed at the (island) Escudo de Veragua on the Atlantic, and at the River Chiriqui Viejo on the Pacific; these limits being recognized and respected by the authorities of the Kingdom of Santa Fé de Bogota, and by those of Guatemala, under the Spanish Government.

According to this demarkation, the Isle Escudo de Veragua belongs to Costa Rica, and also the territory from the mouth of the River Chiriqui on the north to the River Chiriqui Viejo on the south, thus placing Punta Burica in the territory of this Republic.

Colombia proclaimed her independence in 1810, and in 1819 declared that her limits should be the same as those maintained by the old Captain-Generalcy of Venezuela and the Viceroyship of the new Kingdom of Granada, in conformity with the marking off by the Government of Spain, which, on the

Central American side, is the same as has been described.

The first Constitution of Central America, decreed November 22, 1824, declared, in Article 5, that the Republic embraced all the territory which formerly had constituted the Kingdom of Guatemala; and the Special Constitution of Costa Rica, as a State of the Federation, declared the same in the following words: "That the territory of the State extended to the Escudo de Veragua on the Atlantic side, and to the River Chiriqui on the Pacific."

Affairs remained in this condition until the Molina-Gaul Treaty was concluded, March 15, 1825, by which Colombia and Central America promised to respect the limits then existing, and reserved for special agreement the drawing of the boundary line.

Colombia had declared, in 1822, that the Mosquito coast remained open for indirect commerce; and in 1824, having news that projects existed for colonization in the district of Payais, declared it would not consent to the establishing of such colonies, and sent to take possession of St. André's Island; but neither declaration was maintained, nor was the attempt at taking possession carried into effect.

Further, in 1836, with a view of treating with the Central American Government upon the colonization of the Islands of Bocas del Toro, by means of a contract with Colonel Galindo,

"Las Ventanas." A Mountain Stream.

the Provincial Governor of Veragua, Colombia, on September 23d, protested against the occupation of these islands, and pointed out that the Government of New Granada would make evident its authority as far as the River Culebras, this side of Admiral's Bay.

New Granada, supported by the Royal Decree of San Lorenzo, issued November 20, 1803, regarded the bay in question as part of her possessions, and, consequently, the islands in it as well.

The Decree of San Lorenzo confined itself to charging the authorities of Santa Fé to guard the coast, from the Chagres River in Panama to the end of Cape Gracias á Dios in Honduras, having in mind the frequent incursions of the Mosquito people upon that shore. In order to give this Decree the nature of a claim, and thus exact for Colombia a great part of the Atlantic coast of the ancient Kingdom of Guatemala, it was adduced, and with some reason, that by the Molina-Gaul Treaty the boundaries existing in 1810 had been recognized, but no greater extent was ever reclaimed by that Republic than to the River Culebras.

The injustice of New Granada, or Colombia, is obvious at once; because, either the San Lorenzo Decree was a royal title which extended it to Cape Gracias á Dios, or else it was given no authority as far as the Culebras River, considerably distant from the Isle Escudo de Veragua;

nevertheless, giving this Decree a force that it did not possess, Colombia, from 1836, took possession of Admiral's Bay and adjacent territories, all of which belonged indisputably to Central America.

At various times efforts have been made to fix the boundary between the two countries.

"General Don Pedro Alcantara Herrán, a prominent personage in the Spanish-American Independence, appeared in Costa Rica while Central America was engaged in the Walker War, offered his sword to fight the filibusters, and made a small donation in favor of the widows of Costarican soldiers dying in Nicaragua. Herrán remained in San José during that campaign, and arranged with Don Joaquin Bernardo Calvo a treaty of boundaries, which deviated from the line traced on the Molina map. This treaty was ratified by the Congress of Costa Rica, but in Bogota they made alterations, and an exchange was not effected. Later Dr. Don José Maria Castro went to Bogota in the character of Envoy Extraordinary and Minister Plenipotentiary, and arranged with the distinguished Colombian, Don Teodoro Valenzuela, a treaty of limits more in accordance with Valenzuela's ideas and those of Doctor Murillo, the President of Colombia, but little in accordance with the ideas of many other Colombians in office. Valenzuela did not attempt to gain land for Colombia. He saw that Colombia had more land than she needed; a good deal more than she could populate; he proposed to extend the principles of the Constitution of Rio Negro.

"Consequently it was stipulated that the sons of Colombia would be in Costa Rica as Costaricans, and the sons of Costa Rica in Colombia as Colombians, and that there would be the same liberty for the public in Costa Rica as was guaranteed by the Rio Negro Constitution. This treaty, however, did not fix the same limits as the map of Molina gives, which are a line traced between Punta Burica and Escudo de Veragua. Doctor Castro could not obtain this line, for all the disinterestedness manifested by Murillo and Valenzuela as to lands. He could not obtain it, because it passed not only over Colombian settlements, but some of these remained on the Costarican side, and the Colombian Constitution prohibits the ceding of villages. Some of these settlements had been formed in spite of the Artieda Chirinos claims, because the population of Colombia increases and extends, while that of Costa Rica is not augmented in this locality. In order to compensate Costa Rica for what she lost according to the map of Molina, various lines were traced seeking uninhabited sections; but this treaty remained subject to ratification. Castro remained in Bogota combating antagonistic influences, in hopes that the Colombian Senate would ratify the treaty, and when he most had hopes of gaining it, an adverse circumstance came to frustrate his plans. There was a revolution in Panama, in which several Costaricans took active part. This revolution produced a disagreeable impression in Bogota; information was asked of Doctor Castro, who, being completely ignorant of what was passing on the Isthmus, was unable to give it. This failure of his to explain was attributed by some to lack of sincerity and to double-dealing, and the advantageous position of the Costarican ministry in Colombia was injured. The ratification of the treaty thereupon fell through, and Doctor Castro returned to Costa Rica, where he had been working before his departure to become elected President, and in which he was successful. Castro, although in power, would have met with great difficulty in having the treaty ratified in Costa Rica, because the articles in relation to propagating the political principles which ruled in Colombia were in conflict with those which then ruled in Costa Rica."*

Later on, the Colombian Government sent successively, Doctor Antonio Maria Pradilla and General Don Buenaventura Correoso, who, in the characters of Ministers Plenipotentiary,

---

* The cordiality and fraternal sentiments which unite Costa Rica and her neighbors cause us to hope for a fortunate termination of the pending negotiations in the matter of a definite fixing of frontiers.

resided in this country, without altering the aspect of things.

In this condition the question was submitted for arbitration to the King of Spain, to whose court the illustrious Costarican Don Leon Fernandez was accredited representative of Costa Rica.

No decision has as yet been rendered.

ORIGIN OF THE NAME.

Up to the present time it can not be shown how the country was christened Costa Rica—a name given from its discovery to all the Veragua coast.

Connected solely with the Republic, the name is found in the narrative of the expedition of Martin Estete to the River San Juan, in the year 1529; given him, doubtless, by Doctor Robles and Hernan Sanchez de Badajoz, to whom the christening is attributed from 1539. In an official document, with the king's writing, May 4, 1541, the name also appears by which the country is designated, and to which she is well entitled by reason of her rich soil and advantageous position in the center of the American Continent.

The idea that Costa Rica owes her name to the mines of Tisingal, which, it has been said, existed near the City of Estrella, on the Atlantic coast, appears to have originated from a corruption of the name Tiusigal from Tegucigalpa, near where rich mines have been and are now worked.

Lussan, in relating his travels in 1687, wrote Tiusigal for Tegucigalpa, a name which in the translation of his work was taken for Tinsigal, and again, later, changed to Tisingal, a place supposed afterward to be in Costa Rica.

As to the City of Estrella, which has never existed in or near Costa Rica, there was probably a confusion of names between the river so called, where it is certain there exists considerable gold, and some of the villages located in its neighborhood.

ARMS AND COLORS.

It is unnecessary to state that the first flag that fluttered in Costa Rica was that of Spain, and that consequently her shield was that of the mother country; but it should be stated that later on she had her own shield, conceded to Cartago August 17, 1565. This shield was divided in two parts; the first contained a lion rampant, in a red field, with a crown at the head, and three bars sangre, and the lower part a golden castle in an azure field; and for the orle, six black eagles in a field of argent, having for crest a large golden crown with the inscription "*Fide et Pace.*"

After independence, the first flag of Costa Rica was the Mexican, in virtue of her annexation to the Empire of Iturbide; but, as it appears, it was not hoisted, but placed under a load of tobacco dispatched to Nicaragua.

The first flag proper, white, with a red star in the center, was decreed May 1, 1823, and sworn to June 8th of the same year.

Afterward came the flag of the Central American Federation, composed of three horizontal stripes, two blue, and a white one between. Still later, President Carrillo, April 21, 1840, decreed that the flag should consist of three horizontal bands, the top and the bottom white, and the center azure, upon which should be pictured the arms of the State, consisting of a radiant star, placed in the center of a celestial background, with the inscription at the circumference, "State of Costa Rica." Finally, upon the country assuming fullness of power, the flag which we have to-day was decreed.

It consists of five horizontal bars, the outer ones blue, the next white, and the central red and of double width.

The first shield, decreed May 13, 1823, was a star encircled with the inscription: "Costa Rica Free." The second, decreed October 27, 1824, represented a circle of mountain chains and volcanoes, denoting the position and security of the country; and in the center an arm and the left half of a breast, indicating that it gives a heart to its brethren and maintains an arm in defense of its country.

The shield of Central America represented

five volcanoes, and at the left the rising sun; using also for the money an oak-tree, bordered with the inscription: "Libre cresca fecunda" (Free she may grow fruitful).

On the 28th of September, 1848, were decreed the present arms and colors; and since then the shield has been composed of three volcanoes, joined and placed between two seas, with a ship at each side, showing that she has ports in both oceans; at the left, the sun rising, which denotes the youth of the Republic; at the top, five stars, representing the five provinces in which she is divided. Encircling the shield, three flags; on each side, pikes, rifles, and branches of laurel, and at the bottom, a cannon and a horn of plenty for the riches of the country. In the upper part extends a scarf, upon which is inscribed "America Central," and below, "Republic of Costa Rica," denoting that the latter is part of the former.

PHYSIOGNOMY OF THE COUNTRY.

The chain of the Andes crosses it from northwest to southeast, and from this, branch out the mountains which cross in every direction, forming high plateaus, immense valleys, and extensive coasts, dividing the land naturally into three regions: The high table-lands, the region between the foot-hills of the mountains and the coasts, and the vast and fertile coast plains.

The highlands of Dota embrace the central part. Those of Poas and Barba extend a little to the north, and join with those of Irazu and Turrialba, disappearing toward the Atlantic coast.

To the south of Turrialba and the east of Dota rises the high ground of Chirripo, and, in an almost parallel line with the Atlantic coast, continue the mountains of Lyon (Ujum), Pico Blanco (Kamuc), Pico Rovalo, and Cordillera de Chiriqui.

On the northwest side the mountains of Poas are followed by the chain which forms the hills called the Guatusos, the Sierra Tilaran, Cerro Pelado, Tenorio, Miravalles, Rincon de la Vieja y Orosi.

Another important chain extends from the Mountain Herradura until it reaches and joins the great Mountain of Dota on the north, including between the two points the ridges of Turrubales, Puriscal, and Candelaria.

SOME OF THE PRINCIPAL ELEVATIONS.

Peak of Blanco	11,800 feet.
Volcano Irazu	11,500 "
" Turrialba	11,350 "
" Poas	8,895 "
" Barba	8,700 "
Peak of Rovalo	7,012 "
Elevation of Ochomogo	5,265 "
Volcano Orosi	5,200 "
" Miravalles	4,700 "
Mount Aguacate	4,132 "

Thus the principal elevations of Costa Rica are found dividing the country into many and various regions, among which that of the Mountain of Aguacate should be mentioned as notable for mineral wealth.

VOLCANOES.

There are known to be six, whose names, given in the preceding paragraph, are Irazu, Turrialba, Poas, Barba, Orosi, and Miravalles.

These volcanoes have caused no damage of any amount, excepting the earthquakes of Cartago in 1723, 1822, and 1841, the last of which completely destroyed the city.

Irazu, from time to time, gives signs that it is not extinct.

In 1866 Turrialba was throwing ashes up and out for long distances; since then it has remained active, as is indicated by the column of smoke which constantly rises from its crater.

GULFS AND BAYS.

The Republic has on the Pacific side the Bay of Salinas, at the northwest extremity of its territory, those of Santa Elena, Murcielago, Culebra, and Los Cocos; in the Gulf of Nicoya, that of La Ballena and Herradura, with a magnificent harbor; and in the southeast extremity, the great Bay of David.

The Gulf of Nicoya, toward the northwest, and a little to the center, and the Gulf of Dulce, next the Bay of David, offer sheltered ports and secure harbors for all classes of vessels.

On the Atlantic, Costa Rica has the little Bays of Moin and Limon, and the great Bay of Bocas del Toro, between Cape Valiente and the Boca del Drago.

PENINSULAS AND CAPES.

The great Cape of Nicoya, which covers the gulf of the same name, the peninsula formed by the Gulf of Dulce and Cape David, at whose extremity is found Punta Burica, are notable on the Pacific, as are Cape Blanco, forming the southern extremity of the Nicoya Peninsula, and Mata Palo, similarly situated on that of the Gulf of Dulce.

In the Atlantic, Cape Valiente is the only one worthy of note; but there are various puntas (points), among which may be mentioned Punta Blanca, or Portete, north of Limon; Punta Limon, where is the city of that name, and Punta Cahuita, toward the south.

LAKES.

There are no lakes of importance. These, however, may be cited: Sierpe, situated north of the Gulf of Dulce; Sansan, between the Rivers Sixola and Changuinola; San Carlos, in the plains of the same name; Manati, near the Rivers San Juan and Sarapiqui. There are also several still smaller ones, like that of Barba, "El Surtidor," north of Cartago, and what remains of "El Socorro," also called Lake Ochomogo.

RIVERS.

The entire territory is crossed by rivers and rivulets, which render all parts fertile, and supply water-power sufficient to move any kind of mill.

The principal rivers which flow toward the Pacific are the Tempizque, in which are united the waters of almost all the interior of Guanacaste, emptying into the Gulf of Nicoya; the Barranca, which empties at the south of Puntarenas; the Rio Grande, whose outlet is Tarcoles, a little north of Herradura; the Rio Grande of Pirris, the Naranjo, the Savegre, the Baru, and the Terraba, or General, emptying direct into the ocean; and the Dulce, the Coto, the Pavon, and others of less importance, which empty into the Gulf of Dulce.

The Rio Frio, navigable for some distance, empties into Lake Nicaragua, just where the San Juan River begins. There also empty into the same lake the Rivers Zapatero, Viejo, Negro, Platanares, and others.

The San Carlos and Sarapiqui, which are the principal channels of commerce of Alajuela and Heredia, are tributaries of the San Juan. Both flow northeast—a distance of twenty miles between them.

The Rio Sucio divides itself between the Sarapiqui and the Colorado, facilitating communication over a vast extent.

There empty direct into the Atlantic the Col-

Mountain Stream and Hammock Bridge.

Getting Across.

orado, which receives for the most part the waters of the San Juan; the Parismina, into which empties the Reventazon, which rises southeast of Cartago; the Pacuare and the Matina, nearly all communicating by estuaries; the Toro, or Moin, empties north of Port Limon, as also the Penitencia; the Suerte, the Palacio, the Tortuguero, and the Sierpe empty through an ocean estuary at the point called Tortuguero.

South of Limon, the Limon, Banana, Bananita, and others not carrying much water, empty.

The Teliri, or Sixola, which flows for a long distance, and the Tilorio (Changuinola), which is the famous River of Estrella, empty farther to the south, after watering, with their many affluents, the important territory of Talamanca.

Into the Admiral's Bay there empty the Rivers Bananos, El Barras, El Rovalo, and others carrying less water.

ISLANDS.

The Republic has various little islands in the Pacific between the Bay of Salinas and Cape Blanco; those in the Gulf of Nicoya, of which the principal are Chira and San Lucas; the island of Caño, in 8° 40' North Latitude, and 83° 52' Longitude west from Greenwich, and the Isle of Coco, situated in 5° 30' North Latitude, and 87° West Longitude.

On the Isle of San Lucas is a fortress of the

same name, and this is also the case with the Isle of Coco.

The latter is the celebrated island, of which it is related, that great treasures were secreted upon it many years since by pirates, who, being pursued and shipwrecked, could not recover them. The effect of this story about the island was to attract thither numerous expeditions, none of which has discovered more than the earth upturned by those who preceded them in the search.

On the Atlantic side, the Republic has the Islands of Colon, San Cristobal, Bastimentos, Popa, and beside the Bay of Bocas del Toro, the Escudo de Veragua, and the Isle of Uvita; this last in front of Port Limon.

CLIMATE.

The average temperature is from 23° to 26° Centigrade (65° Fahrenheit) throughout the year; somewhat lower in the months from November to March, that period in which nature is resplendent, and when the activity and excitement at the gathering of the harvests present a spectacle full of life.

The climate is remarkably even and healthful; there is no excess of heat or cold; nor are there endemic and malignant diseases; only upon the coasts are there occasional cases of fever. The deaths of children under five years of age constitutes 50 per cent. of the general mortality, which is one death per year to every forty-seven inhabitants; the fact that the death rate is so vastly disproportioned as to children is not from any fault of climate, but rather from the erroneous habits of the greater part of the people as to hygiene, which is also responsible for the slow increase of population.

According to the census of 1883, there were in the country 140 persons or so of over ninety years, including twenty-one who were over one hundred.

SEASONS.

In Costa Rica it usually rains from May to November in the central regions and on the Pacific side; on the Atlantic side some variation is observed, but, as a rule, the reverse is the order. In the dry season, as in the rainy, the sun rises at 6 in the morning, and sets at the same hour in the afternoon.

Tempests, cyclones, and hurricanes, which in other parts of the world cause periodical damage, are unknown; and the rains never bring any danger of floods, owing to the conformation of the earth.

POPULATION.

At different times attempts have been made to place the population of Costa Rica at a much higher figure than it had really reached.

These vain attempts have been contradicted by the results of the census taken at various periods. Although these results may not be exact, they give, without doubt, the approximate population.

From the census of 1826, the number of people was 61,846, much less than in 1813, at the time of election of members for the Provincial representation.

In 1835 the census gave an increase of 12,719—the total amounting to 74,565, distributed as follows:

```
District of San José........................23,606
   "     " Cartago..........................19,700
   "     " Heredia ..........................15,262
   "     " Alajuela........................... 8,930
   "     " Guanacaste ....................... 7,067
```

The number of females exceeded the males by 4,151.

This disproportion was also observed in the latest census, and is due to the prejudice of the people against census-taking, many males, who have not entered the army or who for any other reason have fears, concealing themselves.

RÉSUMÉ.

PROVINCES.	Census of 1844. Inhabitants	Census of 1864. Inhabitants	Census of 1883. Inhabitants	Census of 1888. Inhabitants
San José............	25,949	37,206	56,162	63,406
Alajuela............	10,837	27,171	45,205	51,087
Cartago	*19,884	23,064	30,428	33,887
Heredia	17,236	17,791	25,818	29,409
Guanacaste..........	5,193	10,431	14,902	16,323
Puntarenas..........	883	†4,836	7,700	8,409
Limon..............	....	....	1,858	1,770
Totals............	79,982	120,499	182,073	204,291

* Including 1,075 inhabitants of Terraba and Boruca.

† Including 1,231 inhabitants of Gulf Dulce, Terraba, Boruca, and Gulf of Nicoya.

Doctor Estreber, in charge of the census of 1864, made a note of the fact that in the twenty years since 1844 the population had increased 50 per cent., or about 2½ per cent. per year.

This increase, he says, is considerable, when it is remembered that no change has occurred in the country; that immigration has been small; that the cholera and the war of 1856 and 1857 destroyed at least 10,000 inhabitants; that the years 1862 and 1863, because of the epidemic of measles and whooping-cough, show the births and deaths to be even, and that the year 1861 saw great scarcity of food.

By the census of 1883, the Bureau of Statistics confirmed his estimate that the average increase of population per annum was 2½ per cent.

To form a complete estimate of the population of the Republic, we should add to the above figures the number of indigenous inhabitants of Talamanca and Guatuso, which may well be placed at 3,500.

```
Civilized population......................204,291
Indigenous population.. ...................  3,500
                                          -------
Total...............................207,791
```

CHARACTER OF THE PEOPLE.

It is not in this country as in other countries of like origin in America. In Costa Rica, while a primitive people still exists, its numbers are few, and it is completely separate from the civilized race. The latter is white, homogeneous, healthy, and robust, and to these are added qualities of mind which are most admirable: industry, desire for culture and advancement, a spirit of order, love of work, courage and intrepidity when it comes to defending the Nation.

The morality of the people and their respect for authority is well known; society has been given no cause for alarm by violent deeds or atrocious crimes.

Although at times, in the struggles of political parties for power, arms have been taken up, yet property has been sacred, and peaceful inhabitants have had nothing to fear. Plunder and violence, assaults in villages or on highways, are unknown. Honesty and fulfillment of obligations are among the characteristics of the people, and if its industry is exceptional, no less commendable is its cleverness in business affairs.

FOREIGNERS.

In 1883 there were 4,672 foreigners in the country. Since then the number has increased greatly, owing probably to the work going on upon a new branch of the railroad, from Cartago to Reventazon, and also to the new factories and industries founded in the past three or four years.

In 1883 the foreigners were divided into 1,427 from other Central American Republics,

902 Jamaicans, 570 Spaniards, 530 Colombians, 240 Germans, 219 Chinese, 198 French, 195 English, 130 North Americans, 89 Cubans, 63 Italians, 31 Mexicans, and 78 of various nationalities.

FOREIGNERS IN COSTA RICA.
BY CENSUS OF 1888.

Americans (United States)	250
English	247
French	233
Germans	298
Swedes	200
Spaniards	648
Italians	1,317
Belgians	23
Danes	13
Swiss	12
Dutch	9
Austrians	8
Portuguese	1
Russians	1
South Americans	697
Mexicans	85
Guatemalans	135
Hondurani&ns	142
Nicaraguans	1,208
Salvadorians	184
Cubans	147
Jamaicans (principally colored)	839
Portoricans	11
Africans	2
Chinese	198
Hindostanese	3
Total	6,856

OCCUPATIONS.

Apothecaries	44	Bookbinders	10
Architects	5	Brewers	5
Bachelors of Arts	193	Butchers	268
Bakers	66	Carpenters and cabinet-	
Barbers	67	makers	871
Beltmakers	18	Cartdrivers	1,924

Cigar-makers (males, 38; females, 488)	526	Mattress-makers	12
Clergymen	119	Mechanics	12
Clerks, etc.	703	Merchants, commission men and bankers	660
Coachmen	29	Milliners	19
Confectioners and pastry cooks	151	Mine-owners*	3
Cooks (males, 30; females, 3,917)	3,947	Muleteers	123
		Musicians	211
Day laborers	18,278	Nurses	55
Dentists	7	Painters	29
Divers	20	Photographers	6
Doctors	25	Preceptors	366
Dyers	7	Printers	46
Engineers	13	Public employés	820
Farmers and landholders	7,479	Sailors	70
		Sculptors	4
Governesses	360	Seamstresses	5,834
Gunsmiths	10	Servants (males, 258; females, 2,561)	2,819
Hatmakers (males, 219; females, 292)	511	Shoemakers	358
		Silversmiths	22
Horticulturists	8	Smiths	5
Hotel-keepers	42	Soapmakers (males, 30; females, 112)	142
Jewelers	13		
Lawyers	78	Soldiers in service	505
Leather-dressers	51	Students	17,174
Linen-ironers	890	Surveyors	28
Marble-cutters	6	Tailors	415
Masons and stonecutters	427	Tinners	22
		Washer-women	5,300
Matmakers	77	Woodcutters	214

PRODUCTIONS.

Few countries of the globe are as richly endowed by nature as Costa Rica. Her coasts washed by the two great oceans, the wonderful fertility of her soil, her mineral treasures, her extensive fauna, the variety of her climate, and healthfulness, especially on the

---

*There are five mining enterprises, employing over 250 workmen, besides others engaged individually in the same kind of work.

high lands of the interior, are incalculable advantages. In truth, the exuberant vegetation is the same upon the highest mountains as upon the coast-lands. Among her metals are the richest and most precious; in her animal kingdom are included many species of remarkable wild beasts, also most beautiful birds; and articles like the pearl-oyster, which constitute a germ of national wealth, not forgetting the *Aplisia depilans* (a small snail that dyes violet), which is doubtless the *Lepus marinus* from which the ancients extracted the famous purple of Tyre.

VEGETABLE KINGDOM.

Doctor Polakowsky has said, in his studies of the flora of Costa Rica, that in no other part of America, and perhaps in no other part of the world, are found the vast variety of plants that exist in Central America, and especially in Costa Rica; for although the continent narrows so exceedingly, yet the same conformation of regions of vegetation is retained, and in this territory are found the same high table-lands as in Mexico and Guatemala, and the mountain chain, whose peaks rise in some places to heights of 11,000 feet.

Investigation has shown the flora of the Mexican plateaus and the flora of San José de Costa Rica to be very similar, although the

Cacti almost disappear in the latter region, but it is not determined whether the *flora Mexicana* continue up to the region of Cartago, or whether this latter region should be considered part of another zone; for from Cartago down, the *Coniferæ* are not seen, nor do the queen *Cacti*, or *Piperaceæ*, flourish here; much less in Panama. There are also observed great differences between the plants of Panama and those of Mexico, while many of Costa Rica are common to both floras, some of her virgin forests bearing great resemblance to the woods of Colombia and Venezuela. This is natural, considering that the territory is the meeting-place of the extremes of the North and the South American Continents, which of course affects greatly the variety of plants and of animals.

The *Cacti*, which, as has been said, are scarce, are replaced in the high and dry regions by the *Agaveæ*, and in the humid regions of the virgin forests by the *Bromeliaceæ*.

The *Piperaceæ*, also, are scarce, or not so numerous as, for example, the *Melastamaceæ*, *Bigoniaceæ*, and *Acantaceæ*.

Palm-trees are found on the eastern slopes at 3,000 feet elevation, and at about the same height on the western, particularly in humid valleys. Here flourish countless species of palms, constituting the most noble family of the vegetable kingdom known—the *Coco, Pejivalle, Coroso, Palmito, Surtuba, Coyol, Palmi-*

lera, etc.—all majestic, and valuable to various industries. The *Alsophilæ* should be counted in this group, gigantic fern-filices, splendid as ornaments; the *Zamiæ*, small bulbous palms, very fine for parks and gardens; the *Epipremmum trepadora* and the *Marantæ*, little plantains with variegated foliage.

As for Orchids, so valued in England, and for which the taste has spread of late throughout Europe and North America, there are hundreds of species, some of which are as follows:

Cattleya dowiana (skinneri and alba), Barkeria skinneri, Trichopilia suavis, Trichopilia crispa (Gloxinie flora), Trichopilia coccinia, Trichopilia tortilis, Trichopilia galottiana (Picta), Trichopilia crispa marginata, Trichopilia superba, Trichopilia turrealbæ, Warscewiczella discolor, Peristeria elata (Del Espiritusanto), Odontoglossune schleiperiana, Odontoglossune orestadi majus, Odontoglossune warscewiezen, Masdevallias (various species), *Brassia imondiana, Pescatoria cerina,* etc.

Especially to be remarked is the vast variety of flowers, native and naturalized, the people displaying the greatest love of floriculture.

It does not seem out of place to mention here the *Morus alba* (white mulberry-tree), as valuable among trees giving food to the silk-worm, which is found in the woods, and is easily propagated.

The Government, desiring to utilize this precious article, has given encouragement to a school project for instruction in all pertaining to this industry; as yet, however, the plans have not been put into execution.

Agriculture is the base of national wealth. The division of original property in Costa Rica presents a rare example; and attracts the attention of the many. There are no holders of immense tracts of lands, but almost all the Costaricans are owners of as much property as they can work. It is thus that a population comparatively scarce has been able to cultivate the land to such vast extents.

Before treating of agriculture, it seems well to present here some of the productions of the vegetable kingdom, not confounding those of spontaneous growth with those which are the result of industrious toil.

MEDICINAL AND OLEAGINOUS PLANTS

Are abundant and various; the following are examples:

Ajenjo (Wormwood)	*Artemisia absinthium.*
Balmasito (Little Balsam)	*Palicourea crocea.*
Balsam of tolu	*Myrospermum toluiferum.*
Balsam of peru	*Myrospermum peruiferum.*
Borraja (Borage)	*Borago officinalis.*
Canela (Wild Cinnamon)	*Canella alba.*
Carao	*Juga insignis.*
Copolchi (Cascarilla Bark)	*Croton eleuteria.*
Higuerilla (various classes)	*Resinus.*
Hojasen	*Cassia.*
Ipecacuana	*Cephaëlis ipecac.*
Jengibre (Ginger)	*Zingiber officinale.*

TEXTILE PLANTS—DYE PLANTS.

Mansanilla (Chamomile)......*Athemis nobilis.*
Orozuz (Licorice).............*Glycyrrhiza glabra.*
Ruibarbo (Rhubarb).........*Rheum undulatum.*
Sagu (Sago palm)............*Sagus rumphii.*
Tamarindo (Tamarind).......*Tamarindus indica.*
Zacate de limon (Lemon zacate)*Andropogon citratum.*

In the region south of Cartago are found woods covered with various *Cinchonas* (Peruvian bark), red and white, known as *falsas quinas* (false barks); these may be cultivated, many localities affording excellent opportunities. The *Quina*, in Costa Rica, grows sixty feet high, with a thickness of two yards or more, and, when well cultivated, produces abundantly.

TEXTILE PLANTS.

The best known are:

Algodon (Cotton) ......*Gossypium herbaceum.*
Balsa...................*Bombax.*
Ceiba (Silk-cotton).......*Bombax ceiba.*
Junco (Rush)............*Juncus cyperus.*
Linaza (Flax).... ......*Linum usttatissimum.*
Pita (Maguey) ....*Agave americana and mexicana.*
Pinuela (Cypress) ....*Bromelia pinuela.*
Pina (Pineapple)........*Bromelia ananas.*
Pochote...... ....*Cedrela pachira.*
Soncollo (Pawpaw)......*Anona muricata.*

The *Ramio* has begun to attract the attention of husbandmen and merchants, by the ease with which it is cultivated and its spontaneous growth. This plant will doubtless be shortly a new branch of national production.

DYE PLANTS.

Achiote (Annotto)..... ....*Bixa orleana.*
Añil (Indigo).................*Indigofera tinctoria.*
Brasil (Brazil Wood)..........*Cæsalpinia costaricensis.*
Carao ....*Inga insignis.*

Carmin (Poke)..................*Phytolacca octandra.*
Elequeme....................*Erythrina coralladendron.*
Encino blanco (White Oak).....*Quercus alba.*
Encino colorado (Black Oak)....*Quercus tinctoria.*
Sanguinaria..................*Tradescantia discolor.*
Sangre de drago (Dragon's Blood)*Pterocarpus draco.*
Yuquilla....................*Moranta indica.*
Mangle (Mangle)............*Rhizophoro mangle.*
Moral (Mulberry)..............*Morus tinctoria.*
Nacascolo.....................*Cæsalpinia coriaria.*
Nancite......................*Malpighia punicifolia.*

WOOD.

In great variety, and of excellent quality.

WOOD FOR CABINET-WORK.

Albahaquilla.....................Sweet Basil.
Brasil...........................Brazil Wood.
Canela...........................Wild Cinnamon.
Caoba............................Mahogany.
Carboncillo......................
Cedro dulce......................Sweet Cedar.
Cedro amargo....................Bitter Cedar.
Cocobola nambar..................Nnambar Cocoa.
Cocobola negro...................Black Cocoa-tree.
Cherre...........................
Chirraca.........................
Corteza amarilla.................Yellow Bark.
Corteza negro....................Black Bark.
Corazon de leon..................Lion Heart.
Granadillo.......................Pomegranate.
Guayacan.........................Date plum.
Guacimo..........................Species of Acacia.
Guayabo..........................Guava.
Guayabillo.......................Little Guava.
Laurel...........................Laurel.
Loro.............................Portuguese Laurel.
Lloron...........................Weeping tree.
Melon............................Melon tree.
Moral............................Mulberry.
Nispero..........................Medlar.
Papa.............................Pawpaw.
Papaturro negro..................
Quiebra hacha....................Species of Fir-tree.
Quizarra amarillo................
Quizarra negro...................

Roble	Oak-tree.
Ronron jaspeado	
San juanillo	
Sirri	
Tres hueros	Three-egg-tree.

WOOD FOR BUILDING PURPOSES.

Aguilla	
Almendro	Almond.
Caragra	
Cedro macho	Male Cedar.
Chirraca	
Copalillo	Little Gum.
Corteza blanca	
Cuerillo	Little Leather.
Cura	
Dionto hediondo	
Encina	Live Oak.
Guachipelin	Strong-wood-tree.
Granadillo	Pomegranate.
Guaitil	
Ira colorado	
Ira mangle	
Jaul	
Lagarto	Lizard-tree.
Lantizco	
Laurel	Laurel.
Madera hierro	Iron-wood.
Naranjillo	Little Orange.
Nispero	Medlar-tree.
Nnambar	
Pavilla	
Pipa	
Plomillo	
Quizarra	
Roble negro	Black Oak.
Ronron	
Tiquisirri	
Zapotillo	Little Sapota.

RUBBER

Abounds in the mountains. It has decreased in the more accessible woods by the ignorance of the gum-workers, who have destroyed the trees. The Government has taken precautions against this evil, and has made advantageous concessions for the culture of the tree.

SARSAPARILLA AND COCOANUTS.

The first of the two was omitted from the list of medicinal plants; the second was mentioned as a palm-tree, but without reference to its fruit. These two are natural products, figuring largely among exports; they are very abundant.

COTTON

Has grown here since the time of the conquest. The Indians spun it and made clothes from it. In Cartago there were some small factories that produced very good cloth; but the competition of foreign importations caused the decline of this industry in the fifties. The plant is not cultivated much, owing to the low price at which cotton is quoted and the relatively high price of labor in the country, and also because coffee is found more productive, and occupies chiefly the attention of the Costaricans. Nevertheless, the proprietors of the said factories propose to reopen this branch of industry, relying upon new hands through immigration, and the encouragement of the Government.

THE GRAPE-VINE,

For which there are the very best soil and climate, according to experiments lately made, might be most successfully cultivated. The quantity of wines imported annually would indicate that the culture might be undertaken on a large scale.

INDIGO

Grows well, but thus far its culture has not been great.

FRUITS, RICE, CORN, POTATOES, ETC.

Rice, corn, beans, fruits of various kinds—in short, all the products of the inter-tropical zones—are abundant. The potatoes are considered the best in the world.

TOBACCO.

The tobacco, although exceedingly strong, is very aromatic. It has been widely cultivated, and there is a great demand for it.

In May, 1771, in the factory of Villa Nueva (San José), 302,161 pounds were weighed to be sent to Mexico, and for many years after it constituted an important export; being monopolized by the Government, it has ceased to form part of the national productions.

CHOCOLATE,

Or cocoa, is obtained from both coasts. That of Matina is famous for its fine quality, and was once an important export; later this branch declined, owing to the hostility of corsairs and Mosquito tribes, and also to the difficulty of transportation and the unhealthfulness of the region. At present its culture is again on the increase there and elsewhere.

WHEAT.

Up to 1860 the wheat produced was sufficient for the consumption of the country. It was so energetically cultivated as to reach the finest grade. The rise in the price of coffee, and the competition with California and Chili* flour, drove out the native wheat almost entirely for many years. It has come back again, however, of late, but the supply is not sufficient for the consumption of the country.

In 1885, 3,331 quintals of wheat and 28,914 of flour were imported, representing a value of $183,232, a sum which, despite the excellent lands, went out of the country to pay for an article which the Costaricans know perfectly well how to raise.

CANE.

Sugar-cane, much of which is destined for the fodder of live-stock, is produced in greater quantity than is necessary for home consumption; and, although of excellent quality, it is not exported; on the contrary, sugar of various qualities is imported from other countries. The brown sugar, vulgarly called *rapadura*, which is made for ordinary consumption, is very good. Formerly it was sent in great quantities to

---

*Chili flour used to sell at $5 per quintal; California flour sells to-day at double that price.

Chili, and, in spite of the high freights, this was profitable.

BANANAS,

Of which there are splendid plantations on either side of the railroad all the way to the Atlantic, form a most important export.

On the 7th of February, 1880, the steamer *Earnholm* carried the first 360 bunches shipped from Limon to New York.

In 1884, there were 350 *fincas* (farms) in 2,225 manzanas (over 4,000 acres) of land, with 570,000 feet of bananas, from which, in that year, 425,000 bunches were obtained.

In 1887, the number of bunches exported reached 889,517, the value of which was estimated at $669,544.

COFFEE.

Everyone knows coffee is a native of Asia. Its production, which for two centuries and over reached some millions of kilograms (kilogram = 2.2055 lbs.), in 1859 reached 338,000,000 kilograms (746,459,000 lbs.). The consumption exceeded the production, whence resulted the raising of the price, and, in consequence, increase in its production wherever it was possible to produce it. In Brazil alone, in 1880, the harvest was 300,000,000 kilograms, without a corresponding increase in the consumption; naturally the price fell, and embarrassments, of the countries which had embarked their capital in this special branch, were the result. Coffee was introduced into the country from Havana, in 1796, together with the mango and the cinnamon, by Francisco Javier Navarro, the Governor of the Province then being Don José Vazquez y Tellez. The first grains were sown in Cartago, where still exist trees from which have come all the seed for Costa Rica, and, indeed, Central America.

Much is due to the Padre Velarde, in the matter of coffee propagation in Costa Rica, under the government of Don Tomas de Acosta, who took great interest in agriculture. Its culture was not neglected at the beginning of this century; but no especial attention was given it until the year 1821, in which the Cartago Union directed various methods for improvement and increase in production. So much else was done by the governing Congress in succeeding years, and by Don Juan Mora, that coffee, among other articles, was exempted from duties, and, later on, certain concessions made to those who cultivated this and other plants.

From 1827, it continued to grow in importance, so that the concessions granted by Mora, in 1831, had every opportunity to produce good results.

In 1840, President Don Braulio Carrillo authorized the sale of the municipal lands "Las Paras," with the express condition that they be planted with coffee, the best known

Coffee Curing.

La Flor de Café.

Coffee in the Suburbs of San José de Costa Rica.

methods to be observed, in order that these plantations should serve as models. The influence of this measure was not slight; but the production was not augmented in such a proportion as had been hoped.

During the administration of Don Juan Rafael Mora, agriculture took a remarkable turn for the better, being much assisted by the construction of important roads. The cultivation of coffee and sugar-cane then absorbed the attention of the country to such an extent that, in 1861, 100,000 quintals were exported, notwithstanding the scarcity of labor and capital, and despite the cholera, the war with Walker, and the revolutions of 1859 and 1860, which kept the country in a state of disquietude.

AGRICULTURAL STATISTICS FOR THE YEAR 1888.

	Sown, Liters.*	Harvested, Liters.
Corn	445,818	24,522,570
Frigoles (black beans)	195,853	3,082,547
Rice	72,564	1,975,998
Potatoes	106,909	1,681,477
Wheat	4,136	27,871

About 7,150 manzanas of sugar-cane were cultivated, which produced 550,436 kilograms† of sugar and 6,166,208 kilograms of *dulce*.

From 7,607 coffee farms, having 25,248,686 trees, there were harvested 14,142,240 kilograms of coffee.

From 198 cacao farms, having 56,426 trees, 152,674 kilograms of cacao were taken.

---
* 1 liter — a fraction over 2 pints.
† 1 kilogram — 2.2055 lbs. avoirdupois.

The bananas produced in the district of Limon, for exportation, were 896,245 bunches.

VALUE OF AGRICULTURAL PRODUCTS FOR THE YEAR 1888.

Province of	
San José	$4,893,625
Alajuela	3,623,092
Cartago	2,142,827
Heredia	2,897,646
Guanacaste	1,042,312
Puntarenas	678,123
Limon	1,245,389
Total	16,523,014

From 23,446,278 coffee-trees, comprising 7,490 fincas, 405,053 quintals* were harvested. In the comarca of Limon, 425,000 bunches of bananas were gathered from 570,000 trees.

MINERAL KINGDOM.

The existence of the most precious metals in this section was revealed to the immortal Columbus on his first visit to these unknown regions. On the coasts, belonging to-day to this Republic, the illustrious navigator met for the first time with the objects of the conqueror's covetousness — gold. The Indians wore it in different forms as ornament, and, as will be seen elsewhere, used it in their trading.

Columbus had always a most favorable, though possibly exaggerated, idea of the wealth of this territory, and the name of the Republic doubtless owes its origin to the appellation he

---

* 1 quintal = 100 lbs.

himself gave it, calling it the rich coast (*la costa rica*).

New information was obtained as to the existence of gold-mines through the advance of explorations during the conquest, attention being given to the fact that the natives of Couto, near Chiriqui, and those of Talamanca and vicinity, possessed a great deal of it.

With information obtained as to the auriferous wealth of these regions, when he visited them in 1564, the conqueror, Don Juan Vasquez de Coronado, caused an examination of the sands of the rivers and ravines of the Valley of Duy, and, in the principal river, found specimens of the finest gold in sufficient quantity to assure the wealth of the bed in question. Vasquez de Coronado then took possession of the region, and named the river "Rio de la Estrella."

New mines were successively discovered in various other places; but none have had greater celebrity, of late, than those known as the mines of the "Mount of Aguacate," whose ridges, according to the account of an illustrious traveler, might well be named "Mountains of Gold."

Besides gold, there are found, in different places, silver, copper, zinc, nickel, iron, lead, etc.

Marble and other valuable stones and minerals are found also, among which are the following: Alabaster; alum; clay, fine, of Cartago; clay, fine, of San Marcos; clay, ordinary, of Cartago; clay, ordinary, of the Canton of Mora; quartz crystal; granite, fine and ordinary; gypsum; marble, white, of San Ramon; marble, white, of San Lucas; ochre, fine; ochre, ordinary; onyx; pumice-stone; stone called lapidaria; sulphur; slate, fine; slate, ordinary; silex; tripoli; tobas.

Coal-mines exist, and the development of one, situated in the Canton of Desamparados, has been attempted; but there are reasons for believing that better ones than this are to be found—one near the railroad in Pacuare, and the other in Talamanca.

ANIMAL KINGDOM.

The diversity of climate and temperature, ranging from the burning tropical heat of the coasts up to that of the mountain summits where water congeals, the hygrometric conditions caused by the arrangement of the cordilleras and the prevailing winds, which affect the vegetation, and the fact of the extremes of the two great continents meeting in this region, are the reasons for the remarkable variety of animals to be found in Costa Rica, among which there are species not to be found elsewhere.

"It were difficult," says Dr. A. von Frantzius, "to find another country possessing, in an equally limited space, as many different species. . . . The explanation is not difficult, however. We know that the climatologic distribution of the country is varied, owing to its geographical position and orographic disposition. . . . . The flora of Central America . . . is also of extraordinary variety. In the same way is explained the corresponding great variety of herbivorous creatures, which in turn affects that of the carnivorous, whose existence depends upon the first-named."

MAMMALIA.

Of the feline tribe, some seven species of the genus *Felis* exist in the country; among these, and occupying the first place for their size and beauty, are the two well known in America as the Jaguar, or Ounce (*Felis onca*), and Puma (*Felis concolor*). Of the other five species, three are known as Caucel, or Tiger-cat (*Felis tigrina*), Ocelot (*Felis pardalis*), and Miquero Lion (*Felis yaguarundi*). Their skins are greatly prized, and sold at high prices. These animals prefer to live in the woods of the warmer regions, but are also found in other parts.

Only two species of Canidæ are found, the Coyotes (*Lyciscus latrans*), which live in herds on the high plains of the Northwest, and the Virginia Fox (*Urocyon virginianus*), that is found in parts of the country, in pairs, and does not fear to approach the dwellings of man in search of domestic fowls.

The cruel tribe of the Mustelas, or Martas (Martens), is represented by the Weasel—Comadreja—(*Mustela noveboracensis*), the large, fierce Culumuco (*Galictis barbara*), two species of Otter, and the Skunk-fox (*Memphitis chilensis*).

Five species of Quadrumana exist. The first among them for size, ugliness, and harsh voice is the Congo, or Roaring Monkey (*Mycetes palliatus*). It is found mostly in the north, alike in cold or warm regions, dwelling deep in the woods, in the highest trees. It is entirely black, and has the peculiarity of uttering its cries a little before sunrise and whenever it is going to rain. The peculiar formation of its vocal organs enables it to utter cries that make the woods resound for a great distance; no animal of the same size can equal it in this respect. Unlike the other species, it is a little suspicious, slow in its movements, and of a serious, morose disposition. Because of these qualities, it is never domesticated. It lives on fruits and leaves, and its flesh is not eaten.

The Red Monkey (*Ateles variegatus*) is quite common in the woods along the coasts, and the not very high mountains. It lives in herds like the other species, and its flesh is very good, particularly at the time when fruit is abundant, being then very tender and juicy.

There is another variety of the Red Monkey (the *Eriodes frontatus*), of a dark reddish color on the back, and dark yellow on the belly, with forehead, elbows, knees, upper part of arms, and the four hands all black. It has no thumbs on the fore hands. It is smaller than the preceding species, is found everywhere, and is very much eaten. The monkeys of this species, and that preceding, are easily domesticated when captured young, and are frequently seen in the habitations of both city and country.

The Cariblanco, or White-faced Monkey (*Cebus hypoleucus*), has a black body, and is found on both sides of the range of volcanoes running from east to west; it does not live in the highest and coldest regions. It is also domesticated, but its flesh is not eaten. Unlike the preceding species, it likes to eat insects.

The pretty and diminutive monkey called Titi (*Chrysothrix sciurea*) lives only in the hot regions of the Southwest. It is easily domesticated, and much liked for this purpose, although it lives but a short time in a cold climate. It has a long tail, covered, like the rest of its body, with smooth, beautiful fur. It is largely insectivorous.

Of the bear family there are three species of very moderate size, representing as many genera. The Mapachin (*Procyon hernandezii*), the Martilla (*Cercoleptes candivolvulus*), whose skin, of a handsome chamois color, is much admired, and the Pizote (*Nassua leucorhynchus*), which lives in small tribes. These three are little larger than the cat, and only the Pizote is fit to eat.

First among the rodents is the Tepezcuintle (*Coelogenys paca*--animal resembling a sucking pig), the largest of the animals of this order in Central America. It prefers to live in places where the earth is broken and well provided with rivers or streamlets, being amphibious in its habits. Like other rodents, it lives upon seeds, grains, fruits, and roots, and its flesh is much liked. The Guatusa (*Dasyprocta cristata*) is a little smaller than the Tepezcuintle, and lives only upon land. Its hind feet are much longer than its fore, and, in consequence, it moves very rapidly. The rabbit, also, is found (*Lepus brasiliensis*), the porcupine (*Cercolabes novæ-hispaniæ*), two kinds of squirrels (*Sciurus æstuans* and *S. rigidus*), and many other smaller species.

Two species of wild-boar are found in all parts of the country; the Zahino (*Dycotiles torquatus*), and the Cariblanco (*Dycotiles labiatus*), which is a little larger. Both live in herds; those of the Cariblanco sometimes number as many as 500. These are much warier than the Zahinos, and more ferocious when attacked. The meat of the Cariblanco is superior to the Zahinos, and often forms the principal food of families living away from towns.

The robust Pachyderm, known as the Danta, or Tapir (*Elasmognathus bairdii*), inhabits all parts of the territory; until 1865 it was supposed to be identical with the Tapir; then there was discovered to be a difference between its cranial formation and that of the genus Tapirus of the south of Panama, and the genus *Elasmognathus* was established, characterized chiefly by the entire ossification of the nasal partition. The Danta is nocturnal, hiding itself during the day in dense woods, where it is usually surprised sleeping, hog fashion, in the mud. Sometimes it charges upon the hunter, when it is very dangerous, by reason of its great strength, biting and trampling furiously. The mountain inhabitants make use of its flesh, though it is not very good.

Of the order of Marsupialia, preëminently Australian, there are, in Costa Rica, some seven species, representing two genera, Didelphys and Chironectes. There are six species of the first-named, the larger being the *D. virginianus*, or Opossum, of the United States. It is known as the Bald-fox—although neither bald nor fox—as happens with the *Mephitis chilensis*, called Stinking-fox, which, in reality, is very malodorous, but not a fox. Of real foxes there is but one species, the *Urocyon*, or *Vulpes virginianus*, called Tigrillo. It may be noted that the flesh of the *Didelphys* is a very delicate dish in the United States and in

Guatemala, where it goes by the Indian name *Tacuasin.*

This species is well known, being often found in villages, where it frequently makes its nest in the roofs of houses. To prepare it for cooking, it is necessary to remove the little malodorous glands, submerge it in hot water, and afterward skin it as they do young pigs.

The *D. Californianus*, and the four remaining species, are all small-sized. The first of the five is larger than the others, and differs from them in having long hair, and being black-skinned instead of gray, or more or less dark chestnut-colored. Of the second genus there is only the *Chironectes variegatus*, known as the Water-fox. It is amphibious, its four feet being provided with membranes for swimming. Its fur is compact, very fine, and of a bright yellow, with dark spots. It measures some fifteen inches from snout to tail-tip.

Of the order of ruminants there are two species only of deer, the *Cervus mexicanus* and the *Cervus rufinus*. The first is abundant and very generally known, inhabiting the entire country from the highest mountains to the hot coast-plains on both sides. It prefers the open regions and the natural pasture-lands. Nowhere is it more numerous than in Guanacaste, where it is hunted almost solely for the skin, which is exported profitably. This is the deer so pursued for its liking to feed upon plantations of tender corn and beans.

It is very probable, as Doctor von Frantzius observes, in his catalogue of mammalia of Costa Rica, that the *Cervus femoralis* of H. Smith, a species somewhat near to the preceding, may be found on the Atlantic side.

The *Cervus rufinus* is known as the Mountain Buck (*Cabro de monte*). It is smaller, of a reddish color, and more gracefully formed. It is not as wary, nor is it so fond of frequenting the open plains, but prefers the woods, and never approaches the villages. Its small horns are straight, not branching, for which reason, perhaps, it is called Buck.

Of the order of Edentata there exist seven species, represented by classes differing greatly. The largest, and least known to a majority of people, is the Great Ant-eater (*Myrmecophaga jubata*), also called Royal Bear or Horse Bear. This is an animal very strange as to form and fur. Its hair has alternate rings of black and white, which make it appear gray; it has two wide bands of pure black, which start from each side of the breast and reach up over the shoulders, narrowing gradually until they unite, forming a point on the spine at about the middle of the body. The hair on the upper part is long and harsh, as is that of the tail, which opens and spreads like a squirrel's, and is large enough to cover the body when thrown over the back. It is wholly lacking in teeth, and has a thin head, terminating in a sharp-pointed snout. Lacking teeth, it has, instead, very robust fore legs, provided with formidable claws, like a bear's. It is found only in warm forests, and is quite rare. It has the fashion of sitting on its hind legs like a bear, and in this attitude defends itself when attacked. It knows how to use its claws so expertly that it is rightly considered a beast to be feared. It usually measures some four feet from tip of snout to tail-tip.

The Ant-bear (*Myrmecophaga tetradactyla*) is a smaller species, which exists in the woods of the lowlands, and also those of the high regions. It has head and members like those of the preceding species, but its hair is short, hard, very scarce, and of a dark iron-gray; it has on its long and thick tail but a few hairs, even harsher and farther apart than those of the body.

Both of these animals live on insects, principally on soft larvæ, which they procure without difficulty, with their strong means for excavating and removing the earth. Neither of the two is eaten.

The third species is the Plantation Seraph, or Serafin de platanar (*Cyclothorus dorsalis*), which resembles the two preceding in shape, and also has no teeth whatever. It is as small as a squirrel, has a close, compact fur of light yellow, as bright and fine as silk, and a very dark stripe along the spine to the end of its tail, which is prehensile and covered with the same fine yellow fur. The Seraph is nocturnal, and sleeps during the day, suspended from the lower branches of trees. Unlike the other two species, it is wholly arboreal in its habits. It is found oftener on the coasts than elsewhere.

Two species of Armadillos are known, the *Dasypus gymnurus* and the *D. fenestratus*. The first is called Armado de Zopilote, because of its musky smell, and the second simply Armado. The meat of the latter is excellent eating, but that of the first is disliked because of its odor. Both species are quite common, and are found in all parts of the country. They live in deep caves which they dig in the soft earth (as do the Tepezcuintle and the Guatusa), provided with second apertures through which they may escape if dogs come to persecute them. These curious animals are excavators of the first order, thanks to their strong legs and remarkable development of nails on the fore feet. Being provided with molars, they can eat, besides their ordinary food of worms and larvæ dug out of the ground, corn and other grains.

Of the order of *Cheiroptera*, or bat, numerous frugivorous species inhabit the country, and some of unusual size. Some of the smaller species are fond of sucking the blood of animals, especially horses and mules, although they also attack fowls. They attack the larger animals on the back of the neck and on the back, and, although the loss of blood is of no great consequence, the wounds which remain are places in which the flies, so abundant in warm regions, are certain to deposit their larvæ, thus producing maggots, which, if not attended to, may cause the death of the animal. There exists a migratory species of this latter class, which invades in millions, at irregular periods, the hot plains of Pirris, in the west of the country, and which causes such ravages among domestic animals that the inhabitants of the region are obliged to emigrate to other localities during the plague, and to take with them their live-stock as a sole means of saving them from the numerous and bloodthirsty enemy. Such are their numbers and their voracity, that in a region invaded by them not even human beings are safe unless entirely covered while asleep. In a single night the strongest oxen die of exhaustion like the fowls, cats, and dogs. These cruel vampires make their raids irregularly. Sometimes fifteen years or more elapse without their appearing; at other times they repeat their visits with five years and less between. From what country they come, and what induces their migration without having fixed periods like other migratory animals, are points upon which we have no information, and which may be elucidated only when the naturalists, so few in Spanish America, shall give us the result of their studies.

As to the other species in the country, to which we have referred, it may be added that they inhabit the whole territory.

In closing these remarks on the mammalia, there remains only to mention the Manatee or Sea-cow, so well known on the Atlantic side. This handsome, cetaceous, herbivorous creature, which science calls *Manatus Americanus*, lives on the eastern coast, penetrating into the estuaries and great river-mouths. It feeds upon the weeds and herbs which grow along the shores, and its flesh supplies excellent food for the dwellers of those regions, who hunt it constantly. Its thick hide is serviceable without being tanned.

BIRDS.

According to the latest catalogue published in the Proceedings of the National Museum of Washington, the number of birds reached was 692; and as there since have been added some six or eight, we may say there are in round numbers some 700 species, or about double as many as there are in all Europe.

This is owing, in the first place, to the geographical position of Costa Rica, which makes it the northern limit of the distribution of many species of South American avifauna, and the southern limit of many of Central America; in the second place, to the conformation of the country, so diverse in heights and climates, giving it the advantage of an extremely heterogeneous vegetation, the fruits of which supply abundant and varied food for frugivorous birds, and to numerous insects which are the prey of the insectivorous. With these conditions the presence of numerous species of birds of prey is quite natural. There are, besides, a number of species peculiar to the country, that is, which thus far have not been found north or south of Costa Rica.

The table subjoined gives a clear idea of the number of families, showing the species, and classes corresponding:

Family.	Class.	Species.	Family.	Class.	Species.
Turdidae	4	17	Cotingidae	17	25
Mimidae	2	2	Momotidae	4	5
Cinclidae	1	1	Alcedinidae	1	6
Sylviidae	1	1	Galbulidae	2	2
Troglodytidae	9	21	Bucconidae	3	3
Mniotiltidae	14	36	Trogonidae	2	9
Hirundinidae	7	8	Caprimulgidae	5	5
Vireonidae	6	12	Cypselidae	2	3
Ptilogonatidae	2	2	Trochilidae	36	56
Coerebidae	5	7	Cuculidae	7	10
Tanagridae	17	55	Ramphastildae	4	6
Fringillidae	18	26	Capitonidae	2	2
Icteridae	11	16	Picidae	8	13
Corvidae	3	5	Sittacidae	7	15
Alaudidae	1	1	Aluconidae	1	1
Dendrocolaptidae	15	31	Strigidae	8	14
Exyrhamphidae	1	1	Falconidae	27	47
Formicariidae	17	32	Columbidae	7	20
Tyrannidae	29	66	Cracidae	4	4

TURDIDAE.

Family.	Class.	Species.	Family.	Class.	Species.
Perdicidae.......	3	6	Jacanidae.......	1	1
Tinamidae.......	3	5	Heliornithidae...	1	1
Charadriidae.....	6	9	Anatidae.........	9	10
Haematopodidae..	1	1	Pelecanidae......	1	2
Strepsilidae	1	1	Sulidae..........	1	1
Scolopacidae......	14	19	Fregatidae.......	1	1
Recurvirostridae..	1	1	Phalacrocoracidae	1	1
Ciconiidae........	2	2	Plotidae.........	1	1
Ibididae..........	3	4	Laridae..........	4	7
Plataleidae.......	1	1	Rhynchopsidae...	1	1
Cancromidae......	1	1	Procellaridae.....	1	1
Ardeidae.........	11	13	Podicipidae......	2	2
Erypygidae	1	1	Cathartidae......	3	3
Aramidae.........	1	1	Phaethontidae ...	1	2
Rallidae	5	7			

The object being to supply a brief and general review of the principal characteristics of the country's avifauna, only those species will be mentioned which attract most attention by their plumage, their song, or other qualities.

TURDIDAE.

The blackbird family, so generally distributed throughout Europe and America, has, in Costa Rica, seventeen representatives, belonging to the four classes, *Catharus, Hylocichla, Turdus,* and *Myadestes.* Of these, six are *Turdus,* or typical blackbirds, and the most common of them is the Yigüirro (*T. grayi*), a good singer, like its fellows, and, like them, of modest plumage.

There are five species of the *Hylocichla,* migrating from North America to spend the winters in the tropics. These are small, fierce, and good singers. They have no common name.

Those of the *Catharus* are also five, smaller than the preceding. They subsist principally on soft insects, and are seen usually on the ground under thick bushes. Their song is most agreeable, and they live at great heights. In San José only the *C. melpomene*, vulgarly called *Inglesito*, is met with.

Of the *Myadestes* there is only the Melanops, called Jilguero, or Linnet. This is a favorite, and frequently caged for its musical song. Its plumage is of a dark slate-color, with which contrasts prettily the red orange of bill and feet.

MIMIDAE.

The *Mimus gilvus* inhabits the Northwest. This species, or one very near akin to it, which is brought from Guatemala and Salvador, is often seen caged. It is an excellent imitator, like all the *Mimus*. They call it Sinsonte.

A species of this family, the *Galeoscoptes carolinensis*, is a visitor to the land, coming from North America to spend the winters. It has no vulgar name.

CINCLIDAE.

The aquatic blackbirds are represented by the *Cinclus ardesiacus*, a species completely alpine and lacking vulgar name.

SYLVIIDAE.

The *Polioptila bilineata*, a single species inhabiting the country, is found in the warmer wood-lands of the Atlantic and Pacific sides. It has no vulgar name.

TROGLODYTIDAE.

Of the twenty-one species of this family in Costa Rica, only one has a vulgar name; it is the *Troglodytes intermedius*, called Zoterré. All these little birds are very musical, and if few are kept in cages it is because, being insectivorous, it is hard to feed them. The Zoterré is perhaps the most domestic in its ways, and the only one that nests in the little boxes or wooden houses that, in other countries, are put for this purpose near habitations.

MNIOTILTIDAE.

Thirty-six species, in fourteen classes; more than half migrated from the North. All are vivacious, and of beautifully shaded plumage. They are called, very properly, warblers.

The famous nightingale of Europe belongs to this group. All are insectivorous, and hunt their prey in flight mostly. A few only are vulgarly called Cazadoras Huntresses.

HIRUNDINIDAE.

The swallows are preëminently migratory, and found all over the world. There are eight species in Costa Rica, all called Golondrinas, except the largest, which is named Golondron. Two species, *Progne chalybea* and *Cotile riparia*, build their nests in the roofs of houses.

They are wholly insectivorous; pursue their prey in flight, and devour very large insects. Their ways are sociable and affectionate, and everywhere they are favorites with the people. They are, besides, useful to agriculture, destroying insects, with a preference for the *Lepidoptera* and *Diptera*. Their rapid and sustained flight is admirably calculated with respect to their method of alimentation.

VIREONIDAE.

A family composed of little birds with varied plumage, more or less olive-hued. Only a few have bright colors. All very musical; their alimentation various, showing some liking for small insects. Two species inhabit the country —one the hot lands, the other the high regions. They have no vulgar name.

PTILOGONATIDAE.

The *Ptilogonis caudatus* inhabits the slopes of the Volcano Turrialba, lives in flocks, and subsists on small fruits. The smoothness and beautiful hues of its plumage recall the Cedar Bird of the United States. It is not a songbird. It has no vulgar name.

The *Phainoptila melanoxantha* is the other species of this family. It lives and subsists similar to the preceding. Has no vulgar name. Its plumage is of a lustrous black, with yellow flanks. In size, a little smaller than the Yigüirro (*Turdus grayi*). In this and the preceding species the males and the females differ as to color of plumage. When young, however, that of the male resembles that of the female.

CŒREBIDAE.

This group is composed of small birds of very beautiful plumage, very active, and wholly arboreal in habits. They live on insects and fruits. Seven species exist in Costa Rica; the female differs from the male in color, the male having much more splendid feathers.

The *Cœreba cyanea* and the *Cœreba lucida* are rather indefinitely designated by the name *Picudo* for females, and *Reyde picudo* for males. In the right season they are abundant in the San José market, and sold at a low price notwithstanding their beautiful plumage. They do not sing, nor can they live long in cages without other food than *guinea*—bananas.

TANAGRIDAE.

This family is peculiar to America and the Antilles, counting some hundreds of species, divided into numerous classes, and composed almost entirely of birds of beautiful plumage. One class alone, the *Calliste*, counts a greater number of species, and surpasses in its feathered beauty any other of all the avifauna of the American Continent.

Indeed, the bulk of the great collections constantly sent from South America to Europe, to adorn the hats and bonnets of womankind, are from birds of this family. Fifty-five species in Costa Rica; many very familiar. All live upon fruits, although they also eat insects. Many are domesticated, and prized for their song. They are often caged, and at certain seasons are seen in the San José market in abundance. The following are given as commonly named:

The *Rualdo* (*Chloropohonia callophrys*). Notwithstanding it does not sing to merit this name, it is prized for its handsome plumage, green, blue, and yellow, with velvety gloss, especially that of the male. Lives on ripe bananas only, and does not live long when caged. The same may be said of the *Euphonias*. Of this class it may be said, that though the male and female differ entirely as to plumage, they sing equally well.

The *Casica*, or *Casiquita* (*Euphonia elegantissima*). The male, rich violet on the back; throat, in front, light chestnut; head, beautiful bright blue. The female, greenish, with bright blue head. Sings delightfully.

The *Monjita fina*, or Little Nun (*Euphonia affinis*). Prized for its song. Very small. Male, violet-backed and yellow-breasted. Female called *Monjita palida* (Little Pale Nun).

The *Monjita güere* (*E. leuteicapilla*). A little larger than the preceding, much more numerous, and more generally distributed than any of the other *Monjitas*. The full-grown male is comparatively rare; is called *Güere fina*, and considered as a distinct species. As good a songster as the *Monjita fina*, but less prized in that respect because so numerous.

The *Agüio barranquilla* (*E. gracilis*). Seen until quite lately in the San José market. Lives on the Pacific side, and though not as good a singer as the preceding, is prized more on account of its rarity, and for its being tamer. This bird not infrequently is known to sing the same day after being captured, and to appear wholly reconciled to its prison.

The *Agüio* (*E. hirundinacea*) is indisputably the best singer of the *Euphonias*. So varied are its notes at times, that it seems to imitate; but its song is really all its own.

The *Monjita canaria*, or Little Canary Nun (*E. minuta*), is smaller than the preceding ones, and of prettier hues. It ordinarily appears in the Valley of San José, a little later than the others, from October to the end of January.

Of the *Euphonias* mentioned, only the *Gracilis*, or *Agüio barranquilla*, never appears in the Valley of San José. Those seen in the market are generally brought from the eastern part of the Cordillera of Candelaria, or, perhaps, from Guaitil, Puriscal, etc.

Although seven species of the beautiful genus *Calliste* exist, none of them are much known, nor have a vulgar name. These little birds, like the *Rualdo*, have beautiful plumage, but do not sing worth mentioning.

The *Vinda* (Widow), or *Azul* (*Tanagra cana*), is one of the best known birds, dwelling in every region, high or low. In habits, arboreal; prefers the cultivated country, and likes such fruits as mangoes, bananas, anonas, oranges, aguacates, and figs. A happy and pleasing bird, but no great singer. In color, a bluish green, very soft and uniform, but bright at the wing-tips. Though not gregarious, it collects in flocks in the trees at the ripening time of fruits. Easily domesticated, and if not often kept in cages, it is only because of its indifferent singing.

The *Tanagra palmarum* is very similar in habits to the preceding. Much darker colored, and plumage more lustrous. Limited to the Atlantic region, from Cervantes to Angostura, and to the east of the latter place as far, perhaps, as the coast.

Casique de rabadilla colorada, or Red-back (*Ramphocelus passerinii*). One of the birds that oftenest attracts attention of the stranger journeying through the interior. Constantly flitting from tree to tree across and along the road, the vivid red of its back contrasting with the lustrous black of the rest of its feathers. It lives on both coast and inland, as high as 2,000 feet. It is not known in the highest lands of the interior, but will probably be brought there eventually to be sold for domestication. If so, it will be a greatly prized captive, for besides its beauty it sings extremely well. About the same size as the *Vinda*, but, unlike this, the sexes differ as to color. That of the female *Casique* is dark and modest. They live in pairs in trees; their food is ripe fruit.

The two species of *Pyranga*, the *leucoptera* and the *rubra*, both migratory from the United States, are indifferently designated as the *Cardenal* (Virginia nightingale). They are sold in the market, but are not cared for, in spite of their handsome plumage, because usually they neither sing well nor live long in cages. They will eat bananas, but are also very insectivorous. Excellent singers if properly supplied with the food they like.

The three remaining *Pyrangas* live in particular regions, unlike the preceding, who inhabit all parts. Of these three none have a vulgar name.

Sinsonte (*Zenzontle*) is a name given the *Saltator grandis* and *magnoides*, the only two species found in San José. This name is also given in Costa Rica, as in other parts of Central America, to the *Mimus gilvus*.

Notwithstanding that the two *Sinsontes* in question sing pleasingly, they are not desirable for cages. Their notes are only heard during a certain part of the year. Plumage modest, especially that of the *grandis*. Live in pairs; are not seen on the ground; and, like the *Vindas*, prefer cultivated fruits and nest chiefly in the Valley of San José.

FRINGILLIDAE.

Almost all of this family are graminivorous; the more so, the thicker and more conical the beak. Excepting the *Spiza americana* of the United States, which arrives in the dry season, there are no gregarious species like those of other countries, where they unite in large flocks to despoil the fields of grain.

The canary belongs to this family, also the linnet and the sparrow of Europe, and, properly, the Virginia nightingale of the United States, besides others of fine plumage and agreeable song. Of the twenty-six species in Costa Rica, those that are recognized with ordinary names are:

Setillero (*Sporophila morelleti*). This is often caged and treated, as to food, like the common canary. Agreeable singer, but its song has considerable sameness. The male is black above, with white collar, and the female usually of a greenish hue. Takes its name from the *setilla*, a kind of grass which is grown on the high lands for live-stock feed, and whose seed serves it as food. It lives and nests in San José.

Gallito (*Phonipara pusilla* and *Volatinia jacarina*), two small species having the same common name; frequently seen in the San José market. The first, olive green, with breast and head of dark smoke-color; the throat, and a line running from each side of the beak to the nape of the neck, a pretty yellow. The second, entirely of an intense and lustrous steel-blue, with a small white mark at the tips of the wings. Neither may be called a songster, although they utter some pretty notes. In the rainy season they are numerous in San José; usually in little flocks, both species together; subsist entirely upon the small seeds of herbaceous and gramineous plants. They prefer the marshy vicinities of the *Chile de perro*, when the seeds of this plant are well ripened. In cages they are fed with canary-seed and *setillero*.

The *Passerina ciris* and the *Passerina cyanea*, two very beautiful species, inhabit the country during the dry season; are very docile in captivity; sing well, and are easily kept alive on canary-seed. Not generally known, and have no vulgar name. Found in all bird-stores in the United States. Of about the same size as canaries, and are as lively and graceful. The *Passerina ciris* has all the under part of the body, including throat and flanks, like the *rabadilla*, and a ring around the eyes of a beautiful vermillion hue, the shoulders of yellow-olive, the head ultramarine blue, with a delicate spot of violet. The colors are perfectly separate; they appear as if painted by a skilled hand. The *Passerina cyanea* is of a rich ultramarine hue, more intense over the head and on the throat; the feathers are lustrous as those of the *Passerina ciris*. Both would be fine cage-birds, since to secure them is not very difficult. They are not rare.

The *Come maiz*, or Corn-eater (*Zonotrichea pileata*). The *Come maiz* resembles the European sparrow in its habits, but it is not gregarious; nor does it nest under the eaves of houses, or in little houses provided for it. It lives in pairs, and is scattered all over the country, but nowhere is it more numerous than on the slopes of Irazu, in the "Potrero Cerrado." It seeks by preference the regions inhabited by man, and seems familiar with his presence. It does not fear to enter dwellings to pick up crumbs of bread scattered for it. It nests in the forked branches of small trees, or bushes in gardens and orchards. Its notes are so unimportant that it is not tamed. It does not eat corn, its beak being too small and weak to attack it; but it is accustomed to break off the young blades of corn when first sprouting from the soil.

The *Spiza americana* is a little larger than the preceding, and migrates from North America, during the dry season only. At a distance it closely resembles the corn-eater. It is mainly gregarious; found in all parts in flocks of few or many, according to locality. Causes much damage to fields of rice, of which it destroys more than it eats. Has no common name, though it makes its presence known in such emphatic fashion. The farmers speak of it as "the bird."

Mosotillo (*Astragalinus mexicana*). Species very generally known; it may be called the Costa Rica canary, appearing, in the cage, very similar to that bird. Its song is varied and pleasing, never so piercing and painful to the ear as is the canary's at times. Lives usually in pairs; is numerous in the San José Valley, and has habits similar to those of the *Setillero* and the *Gallito*. Takes its name from a plant called *Mosote*, whose seeds it eats. Female differs in color from the male, and is of a uniform greenish tint. The male during the first year resembles the female, but when full-grown is lemon-colored on the breast and throat, and bluish black on the upper part, with a small white mark in the center of the wings.

The *Astragalinus xanthogastra* is a species somewhat larger than the *Mexicana*, not inferior to her as singer, and of handsome plumage. It inhabits the Pacific side, from Atenas, probably, to the coast. The plumage of the full-grown male is a rich lemon-yellow below, with a mark of the same color in the center of the wings above and below; has a black breast and throat. This species is not found in San José.

ICTERIDAE.

Oropendula, or *Loriot* (*Ocyalus wagleri* and *Ostinops montezumæ*). Notwithstanding the fact that these two species are quite different in form and size, yet, owing to the similarity of their habits and plumage, they are often confounded. Both very gregarious; inhabit both coasts and inland probably to a height of 3,000 feet. Subsist on small fruits and insects, which they hunt for in trees, removing the moss and dirt. Nest in colonies, building their hanging nests with fine, long filaments admirably woven. Some of these curious structures are a yard or more in length, and much wider at the bottom than the top, the bird entering head-first. They select trees most shaken by the wind, either isolated or on slopes, and choose the most flexible branches, where they may swing continually. Often as many as fifty nests are built to one tree. Both species of a dark chestnut-color; the second with smoky breasts, nape of neck, and head, and the first smoke-colored wings only; the tail of both, underneath, of a delicate lemon. The birds of this family are of large size, the male of the *Ostinops montezumæ* measuring nearly eighteen inches from tip of beak to tip of tail, and the male of the

Ocyalus wagleri some thirteen inches. The females are smaller.

Pico de Plata, or Silver-beak (*Amblycercus prevosti*), lives in all parts, but is not numerous anywhere. Prefers brambly tangles and bushes near cultivated land; goes always in pairs, male and female; active and noisy. In color, black; feathers on the body long and very flexible; the beak, and the iris as well, of a faintly bluish white. Is not rare in San José; nests throughout the valley; feeds on insects and fruits.

Chitote, or *Trupial* (*Icterus pectoralis espinachi* and *Icterus girandi*). The two species are found only on the Pacific side; prized by the people of that region for their singing and beautiful plumage. They are often caged. In all the species of *Icterus*, yellow is the predominating color. They are all singers, and their musical powers are susceptible of cultivation. Some *Trupialæ* are seen in San José, in cages; generally brought from Panama, however. Those interested should know that many of the Costa Rica species, of which we have been speaking, common to Guanacaste and the coast, are as clever songsters as any from farther south.

A bird belonging to Don Ramon Espinach, at La Palma, is spoken of, by an authority on the subject, as a most wonderful songster. It runs the scale perfectly and delightfully. Its notes are smooth and sweet as the melody of a flute finely played.

On the Atlantic side there are the *I. mesomelas* and *I. prosthemelas*. Conspicuous on account of their song and their bright yellow color; they are called by the negroes of that region Banana-birds.

The *I. spurius* and *I. galbula* are North American species, and are only in the country during the dry season. Common then in all parts. The boys capture and sell them.

Tordo, or Thrush (*Molothrus æneus*). This is a regular inhabitant, yet only appears in San José during the dry season, leaving at the beginning of the rainy months. It is gregarious, and is often seen in flocks upon housetops, where it watches opportunities to fly down in the patios and gardens to pick up stray crumbs and grains. Its nests have never been discovered, from which it is suspected of having the bad trick, like its North American cousins, of depositing its eggs in the nests of other birds, and causing its young to be cared for by others. These young, thanks to their superior strength, often dislodge from the nests the true nestlings, without the bird mother perceiving the fraud. The cuckoo of Europe has the same habit.

Sargento, or Sergeant (*Agelaius phœniceus*). This species resembles the preceding in its size and black color, but has shoulders of bright red, like epaulets, whence its name. Lives only in the northwest.

Zanate, or Boat-tail (*Quiscalus macrurus*). This bird, so famed as a singer, is found in plantations on the Pacific coast. Is supposed to subsist on mollusks and the like, which it takes from the ground when it is worked for cultivation. It is common in Nicaragua and Guatemala.

Zacatero, or *Carmelo* (*Sturnella magna mexicana*). The species is well known in San José. It derives the name *Zacatero* from its habit of frequenting the *zacate* (tall grass) of meadowlands. Is, however, arboreal. Its other name comes from a black spot, the shape of a Carmelite friar's scapulary, which shows plainly on the bright yellow of the breast.

CORVIDAE.

Five species of *Urraca* are found in Costa Rica, of which only two are mentioned, they being the only two generally known and having a common name. The *Piapia* (*Psilorhinus mexicana*), which inhabits all parts, and the Urraca (*Calocitta formosa*) on the Pacific lowlands. The latter, though as noisy as the *Piapia*, lacks the cleverness, which some suppose it to possess, of talking like a parrot.

ALAUDIDAE.

This family has but one representative, the *Otocoris alpestris chrysolæma*, which seems to be rare, and has no common name. It is simply mentioned as being a relative of the celebrated lark of Europe.

DENDROCOLAPTIDAE.

A numerous family; the birds live only in the woods, mostly in the hot regions. All insectivorous, their mission appearing to be to rid the branches and trunks of trees of larvæ and insects. They are often observed drilling at the trunks and branches of trees, investigating the slightest apertures of the bark and removing the moss in search of food. They begin operations at the base of the tree, ascending gradually in a spiral and always in a vertical position. The tail-feathers, stiff, pointed, and curving downward, of many species, along with their long, sharp nails, favor this mode of progression. When the ascent is finished the bird lets go, and flies, at once to begin upon another tree in the vicinity. The predominating color of this family is reddish brown, from the clearest cinnamon to the deepest chestnut. This bird is not remembered to have been seen perched in a horizontal position; on the contrary, even when asleep it remains suspended against the tree. It has no common name, nor does it sing, but screams loudly enough.

FORMICARIIDAE.

This family is also well represented. Is insectivorous, though usually taking its food out of the ground. Inhabits nearly all the humid and hot plains of the coast; seldom lives at any height. Plumage has no bright colors. In the virgin forests of the hot regions are frequently seen immense armies of ants marching in a determined path, and gathering as they go whatever they find as food, while numerous species of the bird above mentioned march after them and devour them by millions. The name *Formicariidae* is derived from this fondness for ants. They are good singers. The entire family is sometimes known as *Mirlos hormigueros* (Ant Thrushes). There is no other common name.

TYRANNIDAE.

The birds of this family are also insectivorous, pursuing their prey, however, on the wing. There are sixty-six species; many are found all over the country, others only in certain regions. All the species of the genus *Elainea* and of *Myiarchus* are vulgarly known as *Bobillos;* those of *Tyrannus, Myiodynastes, Pitangus derbianus* and *Megarhynchus pitangua* as Yellow-breasts; those of *Milvulus tyrannus* and *M. forficatus* are called *Tijerilla*, or Little Scissors-bird. The *M. tyrannus* is numerous in San José, the *M. forficatus* on the Pacific slope. The latter is different from the *Tyrannus* in having the underside of the wings a vivid carmine.

COTINGIDAE.

Exclusively American; comprehends, perhaps, the most curious birds, as to form and plumage, in all America. Twenty-five species in Costa Rica, divided into seventeen classes. The *Pujaro Danto* (*Cephalopterus glabricollis*), whose crest of filamentous plumes, in the shape of a casque, is unique; the *Calandria*, or Calendar Lark (*Chasmorynchus tricarunculatus*), with its three carunculas depending, one on each side of the beak, and the other in front; the *Carpodectes nitidus* and the *C. antoniae*, of entirely white plumage; the *Catinga amabilis*, with its rich ultramarine and violet tints; and the *Toledo* (*Chiroxiphia linearis*), with its delicate, beautiful hues, and its sweeping tail-plumes; all subsist on fruits of the forests, and only a few are insectivorous.

MOMOTIDAE.

Five species of this curious bird; the best known the *Momotus lessoni*, vulgarly called Bobo (Booby) bird. All very silent and rather apathetic, not to say stupid. Subsist principally on *coleopterœ*, and make their nests in banks of hard earth, digging round and almost horizontal holes, sometimes six feet deep, and wider at the bottom than at the top, in order to give nest-room.

ALCEDINIDAE.

Five Halcyons; all of the genus *Ceryle*. They are indifferently called Fisher Martin.

GALBULIDAE.

Two most beautiful species; live only in virginal forests of warm regions. Extremely tame and silent. Although their size is comparatively large, as they have a straight, delicate bill, and their color is bluish-green, with a rich metallic lustre, the people take them for *Colibries*, and call them mountain sparrows. They feed on insects which they catch in flight. The plumage of all the upper part of the *Jacamerops grandis*, which is the larger species of the two, is magnificently changeable, of gold and fire, and as brilliant as that of the *Colibri*, or Humming-bird. They nest in deep hollows which they dig in the soft earth.

BUCCONIDAE.

These birds are taciturn and apathetic, like the preceding. They dwell in bushes, perching themselves on lower branches, whence they can flit in pursuit of the insects on which they subsist. They also excavate nests in the banks of earth. Three species are seen; their plumage is dark, and they are only found in the warmest regions.

TROGONIDAE.

Of the five species of *Chotacabras*, only one is commonly known and named, the *Nyctidromus albicollis;* they call it the Cuyeo—from its own cry. It is found all through the country. It builds its nest—if it may be called building to collect two or three dozen little twigs—on the ground, selecting spots least frequented in the brakes and cane plantations. If an enemy approach the nest while the female is sitting on the eggs, she, as do certain other birds, throws herself out of it, and flutters about on the ground as if her wings were broken, moving constantly away from the nest and drawing the intruder's attention completely away from the nest and its treasures. The name *Chotacabra* (Goat-sucker) originated from the early supposition that the species were suckled by goats, simply because they frequently visited the herds of these animals in search of insects. There is an absurd superstition, among the country people in Costa Rica, that reducing the bones of the Cuyeo to ashes, and letting a lover place them in a cigarette for his lady-love to smoke, will immediately cause her to return his passion ardently, although previously she may have hated him. The birds of this family are seen only at dusk, or in the moonlight. They seek their food then, of insects, catching them in their large mouths, which secrete a glutinous and adhesive saliva. Their large, prominent eyes, their ways, their dark, heavy plumage, and their lugubrious notes, uttered in the silence of the night, make them the object of superstition. The huge *Nyctibus jamaicensis*, perhaps the largest of the American species, is found in some of the high altitudes.

CYPSELIDAE.

The three species of Black Martins are generally known. They are seen all over, and pass for swallows, in the eyes of the people, and very naturally so, considering the similarity of habits. They fly in flocks, in the high regions, pursuing the insects on which they live. They perch on the naked rocks of inaccessible spots of the mountains, in a vertical position, sustaining themselves with their sharp claws, and resting on their stiff-feathered tails. They rest in apertures of these rocks.

TROCHILIDAE.

This numerous family, which inhabits only America and the surrounding islands, counts over 400 described characteristic species. At all periods it has attracted the attention of the most eminent American and European naturalists, and has been the subject of many published articles, among which is the celebrated monograph of Mr. Gould, the copper-plates of which are unrivaled. Montes de Oca, the Mexican naturalist, says: "Much has been written, in almost every language, about these animated creatures, but all words are inadequate in describing their shining colors, since even precious stones would be dull beside them." They live on the nectar of flowers and the tiny insects lodged within. In Costa Rica there are fifty-six species. They are found all over the country, but mostly in the high plains of the interior. They do not call them Humming-birds, or *Colibus*, as elsewhere, but *Gorriones* (Sparrows). The reason for this is not known.

CUCULIDAE.

This family, like the four following, belongs to the order of *Zygodactilae*, characterized by having two toes directed forward and two backward, and is represented in Costa Rica by ten species, of which the best known are: The *Zopilotillo* (*Crotophaga sulcirostris*), which lives in all parts of the country, preferring pasture-land, where it seeks insects for food. It has a great liking for the *Garrapatas*, and for this reason maintains excellent relations with the cattle; it is no unusual sight to see this bird perched on the back or head of the animal, seeking the insects referred to, which it easily pulls out, thanks to its strong beak. Its nest is a bulky affair of dry twigs, but has its own peculiarity of being lined with green leaves. It lays four or five eggs, covered thickly with rough white lime, which rubs off easily, showing an under surface of lustrous blue.

The Bobo-bird, or Squirrel-bird (*Piaya mehleri*), lives all over the country, like the preceding. It also subsists on insects, and is so tame in its habits as to have gained the unflattering title of bobo (fool). Its cinnamon color and long tail, and also its manner of running along the branches, gives a certain suggestion of the squirrel, justifying its second vulgar name. Like the *Zopilotillo*, it builds a bulky and inartistic nest.

RAMPHASTIDAE.

The family of the Toucans is eminently tropical, and lives only in America. Six species inhabit Costa Rica, of which are the following:

The *Curré* (*Ramphastus carinatus*) lives on both sides of the country; is generally known.

The *Quioro* (*R. tocard*) is found in the same localities as the preceding, and differs only in the color and shape of its enormous beak. Both derive their common names from their song; that of the *Quioro* is very strong, and can be heard at a great distance; that of the *Curré* is the softer.

The *Cusinga* (*Pteroglossus frantzii* and *P. torquatus*). The two species of this name are smaller than the preceding, and their coloring very distinct. The *P. frantzii* inhabits the southwest, the *P. torquatus*, the east and northwest.

The *Curré verde* (*Aulacorhamphus cœruleigularis*) is the smallest of all the Toucans in Costa Rica. Its color is uniformly green, with blue throat, and, unlike the other species, it lives only in high regions.

All these birds live in flocks in the woods, and subsist on insects and fruits, but they also devour tender little pigeons and the eggs of other birds, which they search for in nests. The cellular texture of their beaks does not permit them to crumble their food, and they have to swallow it whole. They toss it up in the air, and hold their beaks open to receive it as it falls. Their constant practice in this, and the lightness of their beaks, cause them to manage this process with grace and ease.

PICIDAE.

The Woodpeckers, or Carpenter-birds, as they are called in Central America, are a numerous family all over the world. They are eminently climbers; feed on insects and larvæ in the bark of trees, and in the soft or half-rotten wood of dead branches and trunks. By means of its straight, strong, sharp beak, it makes deep, circular hollows in the trees for nests. Only two species are seen in San José, the *Campephilus guatemalensis* and the *Centurus hoffmanni;* the other species, for the most part, live in the hot regions on both sides. The tails of these birds not only serve to support them while they drill, like the *Dendrocolaptidae*, but serve also as a powerful auxiliary in their work of boring, which requires strong and repeated blows. For this, they have very stiff and almost horny feathers.

PSITTACIDAE.

The *Papagallos* are also borers, but differ wholly from the preceding in their habits, shape, and plumage. They have a hooked, strong beak, and use it to bore with; but they do not use the tail, which is soft and not calculated for support. They live in flocks, and feed on seeds and young shoots. Their colors are vivid, green predominating. Fifteen species inhabit the country, and represent two distinct divisions—those with the long tail, graduating to a point, and those with the short, square tail. To the first belong the two great *Ara militaris*, or perhaps *Lapa colorado* and *Lapa verde*. Both are easily tamed, but are not great favorites, in spite of their beauty, because they destroy a great deal with their formidable beaks, and, besides, they never learn to talk, and have little grace of movement.

Those of the genus *Chrysotis*, belonging to the second division, or those with the short, square tail, are generally liked, and often domesticated; they are graceful, and learn to talk easily. Three species are preferred: *Chrysotis diademata*, which has the front of the head of a handsome deep tint; the *C. guatemalae*, a little larger than the preceding, with the back of the head ash-colored, and the *C. auripalliata*, with the top of the head yellow. The last-named shows the greatest facility for talking, and is most esteemed. All the species are called *Loras*. There are also two small domesticated species, the *Conurus petzii* and the *Brotogerys tovi*, known as *Periquitos*. All the species nest in holes in trees, and belong to the warm regions.

STRIGIDAE.

There are fifteen species of these nocturnal robbers. They are scattered all over the country, and are called *Estucuru*, or *Lechuza* (Owl).

FALCONIDAE.

The group of diurnal robbers are numerous. Nearly all the types of this great family are represented by the Falcons, Buteones, Kites, and Eagles. The small, or medium, species are known as Sparrow-hawks, and the larger as Mountain Sparrow-hawks—these excepted: The *Falco sparverius*, which they call Chameleon; the *Herpetotheres cachinnans*, called *Huaco;* the Cacao (*Ibycter americanus*); the Carga hueso (*Polyborus cheriway*), and the Eagle (*Thrasaetus harpyia*). This last is the most remarkable for size and strength.

CATHARTIDAE.

The King Zopilote (*Gyparchus papa*) is the largest of the vultures found in the country. It is rare on the high plains, preferring the warm wood regions of both coasts. It is conspicuous for its handsome plumage, and especially for the rich colors of the bare part of its head, and its splendid carunculas. It is much larger than either the Zopilote or the Zonchiche, and these two, if they are devouring a carcass, will retire to a respectful distance if the "King" makes his appearance, and wait until he has satisfied his hunger. This, of course, results from fear, but the ignorant have attributed it to respect, and, in consequence, bestowed the title of "King" upon the bird.

The Zopilote (*Catharista atrata*) is numerous all over the country, and performs important service in towns as a scavenger. This bird deposits its eggs in the earth, between rocks and under loose stones, in unfrequented spots; it builds no nest.

The *Zonchiche* (*Cathartes aura*) is numerous only on the Atlantic side. It prefers, more than the Zopilote, to live in the woods.

COLUMBIDAE.

The best known of the pigeons are those of the species of the genus *Columba*, which come to the San José Valley at the time when the little fruit called Güitite is ripe, and upon which they feed. Generally they are called Purple Pigeon, and are hunted for food. They travel in large flocks, and are arboreal.

The name *Coliblanca* is given the *Engyptila verreauxi*, which inhabits the valley mentioned all the year, and that of *Tortolita*, or Little Turtle-dove, to the *Columbigallina passerina* —two species very terrestrial in habits.

CRACIDAE.

The handsome *Crax globicera*, called Pavon, is found in the warm regions on both sides. It is very terrestrial, and easily domesticated. The male is black, with white breast, while on the female the predominating hue is cinnamon, it having no white on any part. The flesh of these birds is of fine flavor. The Pava, or Turkey (*Penelope cristata*), inhabits, also, the woods of the hot regions. It is not as easily domesticated as the Pavon, nor is its flesh as fine.

The *Pava negra* (*Chamæpetes unicolor*), unlike the preceding, lives only in the high mountains of the interior, and this only to the north and northeast of San José. It is entirely black, with the point of the beak and orbital region of dark blue. Its flesh is good.

PERDICIDAE.

The Quail (*Ortyx leylandi*) inhabits the table-lands of the interior toward the northwest. It frequents the coffee plantations, and, like all birds of this family, is wholly terrestrial. Its white meat is extremely delicate.

Chirrascua (*Dendrortyx leucophrys*) is another species which, in common with four others of the genus *Odontophorus*, may be mentioned for their similarity to the Red Partridge of Europe, notwithstanding there is no relation between them. A casual observer would easily confound the two.

TINAMIDAE.

The *Tinamones* are more nearly related to the Ostriches than any other group of the *Gallin-*

aceæ. Two large species inhabit Costa Rica, the *Tinamus robustus* and the *Nothocercus bonapartii*. The first is found only in hot regions; the other in the mountains of the interior. They are about the size of the ordinary hen, which they resemble in feathers, and they are called, inappropriately, partridges. They live on seeds and insects which they pick up on the ground. Their flight is heavy; when frightened they rise to a little height and fly straight, only to stop farther on. They deposit their eggs, which are smooth, bright blue, and about the size of hens' eggs, in a coarse nest at the base of a tree.

The *Crypturus sollaei* is known in the country as the Yerre.

AQUATIC BIRDS

Are very numerous in Costa Rica, both *Palmipedæ* and *Zancudæ*. The Zeledon Catalogue gives seven orders, comprehending seventy-three genera, distributed among twenty-five families, and divided into ninety-two species.

Among the *Grallatores* are included a considerable number of heron, which are frequently seen near San José, in the marshes of San Antonio, in the Salitral, and Tiribi, in Ochomogo (Cartago), and other places. At the same points, and on all the high plains, the Rock Heron (*Ardea virescens*) presents itself frequently; and in Rio Macho near Orosi, in

Cartago, and in the San Carlos River, is obtained the *Tigrisoma cabanisi*, one of the largest and finest of herons.

The *Nycticorax americanus* is a nocturnal heron of South America, but also found in Costa Rica.

The Marsh-hen, as it is vulgarly called (*Aramides cayennensis*), is found in open lands near still water, and in savannas inundated by the rains; it very probably inhabits Guanacaste, as also the pretty water-fowl *Eurypyga major*, which has been obtained on the slopes of the Mount of Aguacate.

The name Zarceta (Widgeon) is given, in Costa Rica, to the greater part of the woodcock found on the high plains of San José, at the time when the rains cease. In Guanacaste they are very numerous, appearing in great flocks together with other aquatic birds. Under the head of Woodcock are comprised the species *Numenius hudsonicus* and *Totanus melanoleucus;* and by the name of *Pijije* is designated the *Totanus flavipes*, which also lives on the high plains. The same name, *Pijije*, is given to the *Charadrius vociferus*, a bird that is very numerous and considerably hunted in San José.

Of the Swimmers, the *Anatideæ* family comprehends ten species; among them some fine geese, which are especially numerous in Guanacaste. The *Colymbus dominicus* they call Patillo, a pretty little goose of the family of *Podicipedas*.

The Piche (*Dendrocygna autumnalis*) belongs to the lowlands of hot climate; and for this reason, though it may be domesticated and live contentedly on the high plains, it will not survive there, being unable to endure the cold.

Finally, of the Pelican family: The two species generally known are the *Pelecanus erythrorhynchus* and the *P. fuscus*, both called, without a distinction, Alcatraz or Pelican.

REPTILES AND BATRACHIA.

In this branch of zoölogy, the country is no less rich than in others, notwithstanding which, until lately, no formal and systematic explorations have been organized. Professor Cope, in 1875, in the Journal of the Philadelphia Academy of Sciences, enumerated 130 species, divided as follows:

```
Batrachia (Toads and Frogs)......................36
Lacertilia (Iguanas and Lizards).................28
Ophidia (Snakes).................................60
Testudinata (Tortoises)........................... 6
```

Dr. W. M. Gabb, from whose explorations, in Talamanca, Professor Cope took much of his information, discovered that the greater portion of the rocks of this country are of the Miocene period, and that most of the mountainous elevation took place after the cessation of that geological period. The volcanoes, on the eastern boundaries of the table-lands, are of later formation.

Professor Cope based his investigations on two explorations, one by Doctor Van Patten, made in the vicinity of the City of San José, the other by Doctor Gabb, in the meridional region, at the east of the mountain elevation running across the country.

According to Doctor Gabb, the highest point of that part is Pico Blanco (White Peak), 11,800 feet; the highest thus far known in Costa Rica.

In the coast region toward Sipurio, fifteen miles inland, and with 200 feet altitude, is a wide extent of marsh-land. From this point the surface ascends rapidly, so that in Uren, twenty-five miles inland, the elevation is 2,500 feet above the sea-level. The vegetation of all this region is dense. At a height of from 5,000 to 7,000 feet is found the most precipitous regions; rain falls there, according to Doctor Gabb, 200 days in the year, and every day thick fogs occur. Marshes are numerous, and the surface, in many places, is covered with a thick coating of moss. The Pine is not found, as in Mexico, but the highest parts of the peaks are covered with a sparse vegetation, consisting of Artemisia, very similar to that found in the Rocky Mountains of the United States, rushes (Bamboa), fern-shrubs, and clusters of other herbs.

Doctor Gabb made his collection in Limon and Old Harbor on the coast, and thence to

Pico Blanco, being enabled to determine its hypsometric distribution as follows: From the coast ten miles inland, of the *Batrachian* species were found: *Dendrobates typographus*, *D. tinctorius auratus*, *D. talamancae*, and *Bufo auritus*, a coast species. A short distance from Sipurio, were found most of the species of snakes and lizards worthy of note, and the Batrachia *Hyla Gabbii*, *H. uranochroa*, *H. elæochroa*, and *Bufo hæmititicus;* the *Mocoa assata* and *Opheobatrachus vermicularis* come from between Sipurio and Old Harbor, and the *Cranopsis fastidiosus* and *Trypheropsis chrysoprasinus* from Uren. In the higher mountains of Pico Blanco, especially in the rainy region, of from 5,000 to 7,000 feet altitude, are found sixteen species of Batrachia, thirteen of Ophidia, and not one of the other orders. On the summit of Pico Blanco, Doctor Gabb found the *Gerrhonotus fulvus* of Bocourt, the only lizard obtained at the base of the mountains, and the extreme meridional of the distribution of the *Gerrhonotus*, but from the coast up thus far it was not found.

It is especially mentioned that between 2,500 and 7,000 feet altitudes there are found four classes of frogs, with the auditory organs imperfect, only one of which is found lower down. The other three are well known in South America. To this collection was added a species of lizard (*Chalcidolepis metallicus*), obtained from west of the table-lands of the Mount of Aguacate.

Doctor Gabb's collection contains eighty-nine species:

    Testudinata (Tortoises)........................ 5
    Lacertilia (Iguanas and Lizards)................19
    Ophidia (Snakes)................................35
    Batrachia (Toads and Frogs)....................30

Of these species, thirty-seven had not until then been known to science; neither are twenty-six of the forty-six catalogued by Doctor Van Patten embraced in these eighty-nine.

Mr. C. N. Riotte has sent to the Smithsonian Institute a number of species, principally Batrachian, of considerable interest; and other collections sent to Europe have formed material for the study of Professors Bocourt of Paris, Peters of Berlin, Günther of London, and Keferstein of Göttingen. The number of species now known has reached 132.

This we glean from Professor Cope's work.

In the Guanacaste region of the northwest, the abundance of large lizards in the rivers is remarkable. These animals cause damage in the live-stock haciendas, but are not hunted as actively as their great number requires.

FISH, MOLLUSKS, CRUSTACEANS, ETC.

Different classes of these, suitable for food, are found on both coasts, and usually in the rivers in considerable numbers.

The oysters around Puntarenas, though

small, are excellent and in great quantity. The pearl-oyster abounds in the Pacific, especially in the Gulf of Nicoya and Golfo Dulce. In the same place is found the Caracole, the snail that is used for purple dye.

In the rivers flowing toward the Atlantic, especially in the Reventazon, is found the Bobo (Booby) fish, some thirty inches long, and of delicious flavor. The Bobo is caught with net or harpoon; it will not swallow bait of any sort.

ARTS AND INDUSTRIES.

The scarcity of working people and the absence of capital were formerly the greatest barriers to the progress of industry, while at the same time the abundance and relative cheapness of imported articles rendered useless all attempts at home production. There is now a new aspect of affairs; for judicious economic principles have changed the conditions that so long existed.

The lifting of the heaviest burdens of the country, its debts and monopolies, requires years of good government, effective economy, and absolute peace.

Agriculture, allied with industry, must transform the land. It is sufficient to contemplate the position of Costa Rica, in the center of the world of liberty, to realize the exuberant vegetation of her vast acres, and the variety of her natural products, and to understand that in the development of these is the founding of her brilliant future.

Whether the commerce of the world shall continue to favor coffee, or whether this fruit shall be replaced by others, Costa Rica will always be able to compete with any other land on earth in the variety and extent of her productions.

Sugar-cane, tobacco, rubber, textile plants, etc., will come to cover the lands to-day occupied by dense thickets, wildernesses of cedars, and other valuable woods.

The monopoly of tobacco and liquors will not long endure. These done away with, the wealth of the country will rapidly increase, and great sums will no longer pour out of the country to import that which might easily be produced at home.

Following in importance after agriculture, comes the

LIVE-STOCK INDUSTRY.

Although there has been great improvement of late in the breeds of cattle and horses, yet the high grade which it is easily possible to attain in a country of so many natural advantages has not as yet been reached. At different times the widening of the industry has been attempted; now by means of colonization of vast unoccupied territories, now by other methods more or less wise; but thus far Costa Rica,

TABLE SHOWING NUMBER AND VALUE OF LIVE-STOCK FOR THE YEAR 1888.

Provinces.	Cattle.	Value.	Horses.	Value.	Sheep.	Value.	Total Live-stock.	Total Value.
San José....	41,428	$ 634,876	11,881	$174,003	1,279	$9,865	54,588	$ 818,744
Alajuela....	48,561	809,013	11,210	155,407	110	1,028	59,881	965,448
Cartago.....	40,418	778,178	7,233	87,765	491	3,690	48,142	864,633
Heredia.....	26,353	545,655	3,511	60,603	28	162	29,892	606,420
Guanacaste..	94,196	1,304,463	15,580	282,420	149	763	109,925	1,587,646
Puntarenas..	8,712	132,121	1,125	19,892	....	....	9,837	152,013
Limon	2,928	58,125	198	2,932	68	414	3,194	61,471
Total.....	262,596	$4,257,431	50,738	$783,022	2,125	$15,922	315,459	$5,056,375

with immense pasture-lands so splendidly adapted for cattle that they might be raised for exportation, is obliged to import meat for daily consumption. And this, notwithstanding the pursuit of the industry according to the showing of the table given on preceding page.

Under the second administration of Dr. Don José Maria Castro, various animals were introduced, at the public expense, with a view to improving the breeds. The results were most favorable, but ere long the system was discontinued.

Recently the Government has decreed most favorable concessions, stimulating the importation of blooded animals, the National Treasury to pay the freights on the same to the ports of Costa Rica. There is also decreed the founding of a live-stock farm in the lowlands of Terraba and Cañas Gordas, with very favorable conditions for those wishing to establish themselves there.

The cattle and horses of Costa Rica in general are superior to those of the rest of Central America.

In sheep-raising, but little has been accomplished thus far, the industry being but fairly commenced.

MINING INDUSTRY.

At the beginning of this century there was not a single mine opened or exploited in Costa Rica; there was, to be sure, a claim worked

Near "La Trinidad" Mine.

(Las Concavas) near Cartago, and a silver-mine near Escasu, but the work was not pushed in earnest, nor did the claims amount to very much.

At the opening of the year 1815, the Bishop of Nicaragua and Costa Rica, Friar Nicolas Garcia, who had come upon a visit to Costa Rica, in passing along the road of the Mount of Aguacate, observed to a number of distinguished persons who had gone out to meet him, that the existence of valuable ores in that vicinity was very evident.

Accordingly certain members of the party, among them Don José Santos Lombardo, took specimens of the earth, and these being examined in Cartago, the presence of gold and silver was revealed. This was the first intelligence of the rich mines in that vicinity, and it aroused the curiosity and avarice of many sufficiently to induce them to explore that region.

Thus it was that at the end of the year 1820, Lombardo and his brother, Don José Rafael Gallegos, presented themselves before the Spanish authorities and claimed the mine known to-day as that of the *Sacra familia* (Holy Family). Not long after, the Rev. Don Miguel Bonilla claimed the mine of *San Miguel;* and, after the Independence, claim was made to the third mine of those in the Mount of Aguacate. This last was the famous Castros mine, owned by Nicolas and Pio Castro, also by the sons of the first Don Vicente and Don José Antonio Castro.

Everything in this line was rudimentary at that time, and these discoveries would have availed but little had there not arrived at Costa Rica various foreigners, some of them attracted by the discoveries, others fleeing from the convulsions which agitated other Central and South American countries. To some of these are due the first ideas that were followed out, and the first important steps taken in regard to working the mines. One had then to struggle with all sorts of difficulties; lack of skilled labor, of needful appliances, of roads, of quicksilver, etc. It was thus that the working of the mines, besides being difficult, did not yield adequate profits. By degrees they were provided with what was indispensable and most necessary, and at last the mining industry became, and was for some years, the most profitable in the country. The production of gold reached considerable amounts, but as there was no Mint, but little means of communication, and very slight mercantile relations, the bullion had to be sold at low prices to a few speculators, who exported it generally to Jamaica, in exchange for articles of consumption, and for coined gold and silver.

The Mint and Exchange was established in 1830, the country being greatly benefited thereby, and a stronger impulse given to mining.

TABLE SHOWING NAME AND SITUATION OF THE PRINCIPAL MINES AND THEIR METALS.

Name.	Canton.	Situation.	Class of Minerals.
La Trinidad	Esparza	Upper end of River Ciruelitas.	Gold and Silver.
Sacra Familia	Alajuela	Mount of Aguacate	Gold and Silver.
La Union	Puntarenas	Banks of River Seco	Gold and Silver.
La Minita	Alajuela	Mount of Aguacate	Gold and Silver.
Mina de los Castro	Alajuela	Corralillo	Gold and Silver.
San Rafael	Alajuela	Corralillo	Gold and Silver.
Mina de los Oreamuno	Alajuela	Corralillo	Gold and Silver.
Quebrada-Honda	Alajuela	Quebrada Honda	Gold and Silver.
Machuca	Alajuela	Corralillo	Gold and Silver.
Trinidad del Aguacate	Alajuela	Corralillo	Gold and Silver.
Peña Grande	San Ramon	Hill of San Ramon	Gold and Silver.
Mina de Acosta	San Ramon	Banks of River Jesus	Gold and Silver.
Las Concavas	Cartago	Banks of River Agua-Caliente	Copper.
Palmares	San Ramon	Cordillera of Aguacate	Gold, Silver and Lead
Mancuerna	Sardinal	Sardinal Coast	Copper.
Mata-Palo	Sardinal	Sardinal Coast	Copper.
Puerta de Palacio	Sardinal	Sardinal Coast	Copper.
Hoja Chiques	Sardinal	Sardinal Coast	Copper.
Chapernal	Sardinal	Sardinal Coast	Copper.

The existence of many other rich mines in the southern and other parts of the Republic is well known.

The total production of the mines of Monte del Aguacate from 1821 to 1844 is estimated at some $6,000,000 to $7,000,000, a sum which may seem exaggerated to anyone who does not consider that the greater part of the gold and silver was, for want of other facilities, exported in bars, not only during the first decade, but during the rest of the time cited. The Mint and Exchange received a small amount, but the greater part continued to be exported at good prices. Among the companies organized to work the mines may be mentioned the Anglo-Costarican, formed in England in 1834, and the Monte del Aguacate Company, formed in 1868 in Costa Rica, with a capital of $500,000, of which something more than half was made active. The product of the gold-mines in the Province of Puntarenas amounted to $37,496 for the year 1888.

MANUFACTORIES.

The National Liquor Factory is the most important industrial establishment in the Republic. With fine buildings and complete machinery, the results of its products for the year 1888 amounted to $1,136,853.44.

The alcohol, rum, and other liquors made there have obtained high verdicts on various occasions when exhibited in other countries. At the same time, the clandestine distillation of liquors is very general, and their consumption is estimated as being equal to, if not greater than, that of the national liquors, notwithstanding the vigilance of the authorities.

The capacity of the National Factory, with the auxiliaries it possesses, would be sufficient to supply all Central America.

The San José Foundry and the National Workshops are valuable institutions, and have contributed vastly to the progress of mechanical arts. All kinds of foundry, iron, and cabinet-work can be performed; machines and farming tools and implements are made.

The first of these institutions was founded in 1866, by Don Joaquin Fernandez; it has no equal in Central America, and has competed favorably with the second in spite of the latter's auxiliaries. In the latter, a complete locomotive for the railroad's use has been built by Don Manuel V. Dengo, a young Costarican, and a small steamboat by Don Eduardo Chamberlain.

The three beer breweries produce a good article, which has a vast consumption; nevertheless, beer is also imported. In 1884, 6,666 barrels, valued at $49,436.80, were brought into the country, and in 1885, 6,420, valued at $55,956, which would indicate a good field for new manufacturers.

The oil factory, not long established, is busy and prosperous. The proprietor, Don Carlos Volio Tinoco, employs all possible methods to augment the production of oleaginous seeds, a branch of agriculture which was formerly hardly known.

Soap is manufactured for ordinary use. There are factories for this, and many for making candles; but both products are imported in great quantities, and exceed the native articles in quality.

In the factories of Don Federico Velarde and the Messrs. Röver and Prestinary, the machinery for weaving is imported from Europe, and is of the latest pattern.

WORKSHOPS.

Tailoring, shoemaking, belt-making, cabinet-making, carpentering, iron and foundry work, are all very advanced.

Masons and stonecutters are, as a rule, clever at their work. Many have gone from Costa Rica to neighboring countries, having been especially sent for.

The silversmith's trade, and the jeweler's and watchmaker's, have reached great perfection. Not a few workmen, at the first of the three trades mentioned, have distinguished themselves by skill and good taste.

Engravers are not numerous, but there are some, who engrave the dies for the Mint, whose work is extremely fine.

Of gardeners and fruit-growers there are a good many, particularly in San José, where the flower and vegetable trade is improving every day. There are gardens and orchards worthy of note, which produce the year round.

Makers of fire-works are not lacking who know the chemical and artistic combinations necessary to produce the finest pyrotechnical displays.

There are many dressmaking shops.

It may be noted that, notwithstanding the activity perceptible in branches of industry, there is not, in any one branch, enough production to equal the consumption of the article produced. The number of industrial workers is small in proportion to that of the agricultural.

Industries are divided as follows:

Armories	7
Bakeries	18
Barber Shops and Hair Cutters	52
Belt Factories	23
Curing of Coffee—with Machinery	252
Breweries	3
Dyeing Establishments	7

FACTORIES.

Cotton and Woolen	2
Ice	2
Liquors (National)	1
Oils	1
Park System—Remington—(National)	1
Soap and Candles	5
Starch	1
Flour Mills	1
Foundries	2
Kilns for making Bricks and Tiles	117
Lime-Kilns	31
Saw and Planing Mills	72
Shoe Shops	89

FACTORIES CONTINUED.

Silversmiths	18
Other Smiths	58
Sugar-cane Mills (iron)	438
Sugar-cane Mills (wood)	612
Sugar Refineries	9
Tanneries	19

WORKSHOPS.

Carpentering and Cabinet-making	125
Dressmaking	5
Photographing	2
Sculpturing (one in marble)	2
Tailoring	97
Watchmaking	12

The salary of a good workman, from the day laborer to the fine artisan or mechanic, varies from $1 to $5 per day of ten working hours; wages which, in proportion to his expenses, permit him to save—the cost of living being comparatively cheap.

The scarcity of labor requires thousands of hands to be brought into the country, who find lucrative employment.

The factories and workshops in Costa Rica, in the year 1888, were distributed as follows:

San José	836
Alajuela	701
Cartago	193
Heredia	272
Guanacaste	188
Puntarenas	89
Limon	20
Total	2,299

FINE ARTS.

Music has made the most progress, perhaps, and this in spite of the fact that its study has not been general for very many years. To-day there

Shoeing an Ox.

are many good native professors; and instruction on the piano and in singing are indispensable in the schools for girls and young ladies.

Of drawing and painting the same may be said. In these branches there is marked progress, and a great deal of promise is shown by the youth of Costa Rica.

COMMERCE.

At the beginning of the Colonial Government, the Port of Suerre, on the Atlantic, had some commercial importance; but that of the Port of Rivera, on the west coast of the Gulf of Nicoya, was greater; also that of Coronado del Norte, of the Island of Caño, and the Golfo de Ossa, now Golfo Dulce. All the ships plying between Mexico, Panama, Peru, and neighboring ports, rode at anchor at the Island of Caño. It is not to be supposed that they imported other than the most indispensable articles, such as clothing and shoes, which sometimes were wholly lacking. The most important epoch of commerce in those times was that of the extinct City of Santiago de Talamanca, whence cargoes were sent in three days' time to Porto Bello. This people exported cocoa, potatoes, honey, wax, sarsaparilla, and hemp, and, it is natural to suppose, the gold which we are assured abounded in those regions. The destruction of the city ruined the commerce, of course.

In 1638, the opening of the Matina Road was the beginning of a new epoch. The cocoa haciendas of that valley took a new importance; at the same time the Gulf of Nicoya became the center of commerce. The Province, then, was in a flourishing condition, and would have progressed finely but for the pirates and Mosquito Indians, who constantly menaced its welfare, and whose vandalism destroyed the coast settlements.

After that period Costa Rica was reduced to woful misery, carrying on an insignificant commerce, by mules, overland, with Panama, and some few articles of little account with Nicaragua. Thus passed more than a century.

The Gautemala authorities seemed constantly engaged either in not protecting or in restraining the progress of this section, as various official acts will show. Even in the present century (1813) the Captaincy General appears restricting the commerce of the Province more than before. It is known that the colonies could treat only with Spain. At the time of Independence the situation of Costa Rica, if not wretched, was at least sad enough.

Just beginning a political career, struggling to implant a system of government wholly new, and opposed to the preceding one, struggling also with poverty, in a state of complete upheaval, the work undertaken by the forefathers of the present Costaricans was immense;

but under a just government, measures were undertaken for the welfare of the country. By a sure route, though slowly, the march has been upward and onward.

The coffee-culture, as we have seen, has given impulse and importance to Costa Rica, and has begun to figure in the statistics of the commercial nations of the world.

In the forties, commerce was held through Matina and Sarapaqui with the North, and through Caldera on the Pacific; but the difficulties of communication by the Atlantic coast, and the facilities presented by the Pacific, especially when a line of steamers was established connecting with the Panama Railroad, thus opening a new way to the Atlantic, turned the course of business to Puntarenas, a new port which soon became the sole commercial route.

This condition of things continued for many years, increasing the expense of importations, until the Port of Limon was opened to commerce; then the competition of two routes, and the facilities of the railroad and new wagon-road to the Atlantic, decreased the difficulties of traffic to the benefit of the general wealth.

This came about precisely at the time when the price of coffee declined, for which reason this important progress has not been estimated at its full value, the great reductions in freights not being able to compensate for the difference in the quotations of the product.

In 1858, the freight on coffee by steamer to Panama alone cost ⅝ cent per pound, American gold.

In 1860, for shipments of freight of twenty tons or less to San Francisco, 2⅜ cents per pound; and in greater quantity, 2¼ cents per pound, same kind of money.

The shipments to Europe were usually by sailing vessel around Cape Horn. In 1870, the West India and Pacific Company's steamers received as freights:

From Puntarenas to Liverpool, £5 10s. 0d. per ton.
"   "   " London,   £6 2s. 6d.   "

And the English Royal Mail,

From Puntarenas to Southampton, £5 15s. per ton.

While now are paid:

From Puntarenas to European ports, £4 per ton.
"   Limon   "   "   "   £2   "

In like proportion, the passenger rates have decreased.

In 1848, seventy vessels entered Puntarenas, with a total of 7,180 tons; in 1884, this number increased to 113, with 137,368 tons; and in the same year, by way of Limon, 121 vessels, with 126,875 tons. The total in 1888 was 234 vessels, with 264,243 tons of freight.

The total number of large vessels entering the Port of Limon during the year 1888 was 152, while during the same year 125 entered the Port of Puntarenas, making a total of 277 for the year.

COFFEE EXPORTED BY COSTA RICA DURING 1886 AND 1887.

Destination.	1886 Ports Puntarenas. Kilograms.	1886 Ports Limon. Kilograms.	1886 Quantity. Kilograms.	1886 Value.	1887 Ports Puntarenas. Kilograms.	1887 Ports Limon. Kilograms.	1887 Quantity. Kilograms.	1887 Value.
England	2,593,570	2,761,115	5,354,685	$1,388,671	4,622,167	3,091,094	7,713,261	$3,084,303
Germany	879,221	448,882	1,328,103	332,025	382,658	215,939	598,597	239,438
France	83,268	769,508	852,776	213,194	214,842	393,586	608,428	243,371
Denmark	......	171,216	171,216	112,804	......	1,798	1,798	719
Holland	......	5,715	5,715	1,429	......	......	......	......
Spain	......	......	......	......	785	......	785	314
New York	54,086	527,929	582,015	145,504	115,201	2,055,705	2,170,906	868,363
New Orleans	......	9,004	9,004	2,251	......	138,583	138,583	55,413
Boston	......	......	......	......	......	128,975	128,975	51,590
S. Francisco	633,790	......	633,790	158,448	1,635,005	......	1,635,005	654,002
Colombia	55,343	8,606	63,949	15,887	57,062	27,765	84,827	83,990
CentAmerica	2,185	240	2,425	606	226	......	226	91
Mexico	4,352	......	4,352	1,088	......	......	......	......
Chili	29,020	......	29,020	7,255	......	......	......	......
Canada	......	......	......	......	......	580	580	232
Total	4,334,835	4,702,215	9,037,050	$2,259,262	7,027,946	6,053,975	13,081,921	$5,231,766

REPUBLIC OF COSTA RICA.

COFFEE EXPORTATION—1888.

Exported to	Ports by which Exported. Puntarenas. Kilograms.	Limon. Kilograms.	Total Kilograms.	Value.
England	5,498,308	626,298	6,124,606	$2,859,896
Germany	561,729	29,910	591,639	279,763
France	359,145	31,050	390,195	165,002
New York	413,950	1,448,542	1,862,492	819,809
New Orleans		13,452	13,452	6,230
San Francisco	1,235,535		1,235,535	569,881
Colombia	79,212	8,326	87,538	38,329
Chili	7,625		7,625	8,343
Total	8,155,504	2,157,578	10,313,082	$4,742,253

COMMERCE.

COMMERCIAL MOVEMENT FOR PAST THREE YEARS.

Countries.	1886. Importation.	1886. Exportation.	1887. Importation.	1887. Exportation.	1888. Importation.	1888. Exportation.
United States	$1,010,490	$1,028,080	$1,440,729	$2,478,801	$1,798,877	$2,077,815
England	1,878,886	1,489,680	1,771,466	3,125,125	1,649,402	2,884,161
Germany	582,109	835,269	815,729	250,520	833,883	294,391
France	884,946	214,957	612,076	246,350	506,510	165,028
Spain	42,247	......	32,750	814	48,892	......
Italy	......	......	4,608	......	11,566	......
Belgium	6,044	......	997	......	5,659	......
Denmark	......	42,804	......	719	......	......
Holland	......	1,429	......	232	......	......
Canada	425	1,088	510	7,287	1,147	550
Mexico	4,789	87,290	798,665	67,659	64,625	89,019
Colombia	14,469	......	21,741	......	80,642	......
Ecuador	9,600	......	......	......	445	......
Peru	......	7,255	......	......	......	......
Chili	......	......	......	......	60,276	3,843
Cuba	......	......	......	......	......	......
Central America	103,646	138,005	101,054	59,556	149,999	249,990
Total	$3,587,651	$3,225,807	$5,601,225	$6,286,563	$5,201,992	$5,718,792

The principal national products exported during the year 1888 were as follows: Bananas, coffee, rubber, indigo, hides, stuffed birds, cacao, mother-of-pearl, tortoise-shell, various woods, gold in bars, pearls, medicinal plants, and orchids, potatoes, sarsaparilla, rice, cocoa-nuts, dried bananas, and live-stock. Total value of exportations, $5,713,792.

IMPORTATIONS.

The commerce of Costa Rica is chiefly maintained with England, the United States, France, and Germany. The principal importations are silk, wool, linen, and cotton; machinery, appliances and tools for agriculture and various arts; furniture, glassware, tinware, hardware, and haberdashery; articles of ornament and luxury, silk mercery, and perfumery; beer, wines, and liquors of all kinds; soap and coffee-sacks; flour, sugar, and canned goods; ready-made clothing, shoes, saddles, harnesses, and other articles of the kind; books, office fixtures, scientific instruments, etc., etc.

In 1850, the value of importations was estimated at $1,000,000, equal to that of the exportations.

Foreign steamers are free of tonnage, and only pay $25 for right of entry and departure. Véssels that are not steamers pay 25 cents per ton for registry, which goes to benefit the marine hospital, and $10 for right of entry and departure. Sailing vessels for lightering or loaded with coal are exempt from tonnage duty. Men-of-war, merchant vessels touching regularly in any of the ports, and vessels obliged to touch by special conditions of navigation, are also exempt from this duty.

All goods for Costa Rica should come accompanied by a corresponding invoice. The general Custom House is at the Capital. There are also Custom officers at Puntarenas, Limon, and Carrillo, where goods may be examined and all formalities complied with.

In not too grave cases of contraband goods, fraud, or infraction of the country's Custom laws, two courses may be pursued. In the first, as in grave cases, the Judge of Hacienda shall be acquainted, according to the laws; in the second, the Administrator of Customs shall proceed and pass judgment. An appeal may be taken from his judgment to the "Jurado Comercial" (Commercial Jury), which shall consist of the Under Secretary of Hacienda, and of two merchants selected from twenty who are appointed yearly by the Ministry of Hacienda.

The custom duties are paid half down, and half within three months' time.

San José City has fourteen importing houses on a large scale. There are also in the Capital eleven commission firms, six representing considerable capital, and of high standing.

The total value of importations for the year 1888 was $5,201,922.

BANKING HOUSES.*

The principal are: The Anglo-Costarricense, established in 1863; the Bank of Costa Rica, established in 1867; the Union Bank, established in 1877.

The Bank of Costa Rica was formerly the National Bank. The charters of these institutions permit the reception of new capital at any time. The usual interest on money in Costa Rica is 1 per cent. per month, but on such short credit that, although the usefulness of the institutions is unquestionable, they nevertheless have not been great auxiliaries to agriculture and industry. The Union Bank, bettering its system somewhat, has reduced the interest to 9 per cent. per annum.

MISCELLANEOUS SOCIETIES.

The spirit of association has not progressed in Costa Rica in proportion to its business activity.

The capitalists prefer lending out their money at interest or putting it into coffee. Of the banks, the Union and the Anglo-Costarricense belong to corporations; the Costa Rica has become the property of a single merchant, who proposes to give it the benefit of new capital.

---

* The first bank of Central America was established in Costa Rica in 1857, by Crisanto Medina; but it had not a long existence.

Don Mauro Fernandez, Secretary of the Treasury.

MONEYS, WEIGHTS, AND MEASURES.

Other associations are the following: The Agency Company, which engages in all operations of embarking, disembarking, receiving, and dispatching merchandise, of loading vessels, and of the agency of navigation lines. Its capital is $100,000, and it pays yearly dividends of from 15 to 20 per cent. The San José Market, capital $215,000, pays monthly dividends of from 1 to 1½ per cent. The Monte de Aguacate Mining Company, capital $500,000, is negotiating toward reorganization, on a new basis, with foreign capitalists. The Bella Vista Thermal Bath Company, of Cartago, capital $100,000, which was formed recently. The Tramway Companies in San José, Cartago, and Heredia; the Market Companies of the two latter cities, and the Costa Rica Railway, of which we shall speak presently.

MONEYS, WEIGHTS, AND MEASURES.

After the Independence, the first disposition as to money was that of the Junta Gubernatira, of May 13, 1823, which provided for the stamping of gold coins with the value of $16 per onza (ounce), $8 per half-onza, and $4 per quarter; and for silver, 8 reales (American shillings, 12½ cents) per onza. The Government was to prescribe measures toward a Mint for the coinage of round money, similar to that of Guatemala and Mexico.

The following die was established: On one

side, a star in the center, and in the border "Costa Rica Free;" on the other, a palm in the center, crossed with a sword, a gun with bayonet, and a cannon below, and in the border, its value, alloy, and name of the engraver. Later on the die of the Federation was adopted.

According to a decree of December 1, 1841, an onza of gold became worth $18; by decree of April 14, 1842, again $16; and by decree of March 26, 1843, $17, at which it remained.

The ounce is divided into half-ounces, quarters, *escudos*, or eighths, and *medios escudos*, sixteenths. The silver *peso*, or dollar, is divided into halves, quarters, *reales* (eighths), *medios* (sixteenths), and cuartillos (thirty-seconds). The real is 12½ cents, the *medio* 6¼, and the cuartillo 3⅛.

By decree of September 28, 1848, the die represented the coat of arms bordered with the words " Republic of Costa Rica," and the year of its coinage, for one side; and for the reverse, the gold coin contained an Indian woman standing, armed with bow, arrows, and quiver, resting on the left arm against a pedestal, with the inscription "15th September, 1821;" and for the border, "America Central," with the engraver's initials. The reverse of the silver coins contained an oak, with the same border as the preceding.

The moneys coined since 1864 do not have the Indian woman; and their value, arranged by the decimal system, is as follows: Gold, $10, $5, $2, $1. Silver, 50-cent piece, 25 cents, 10 cents, 5 cents. Copper, 1 cent, ¼ cent.

The gold is worth 9 per cent. less than English, and 12½ per cent. less than the United States gold. The paper money of the country circulates in bills to the value of $100, $50, $25, $10, $5, $2 and $1.

TABLE SHOWING VALUE OF MONEYS COINED FROM 1829 TO 1886.

GOLD.

Onzas	1830 to 1834	$188,634.00
Half-onzas	1830 " 1858	283,976.00
Quarter-onzas	1829 " 1863	514,829.25
Eighth-onzas (Escudos)	1829 " 1857	146,862.00
Sixteenth-onzas (Medios Escudos)	1832 " 1864	94,452.12½

GOLD, DECIMAL.

$10	1870 to 1876	580,790.00
5	1867 " 1876	385,490.00
5¼*	in 1874	37,427.50
2	1866 to 1876	30,432.00
1	1864 " 1872	88,915.00

Total............$2,351,807.87½

SILVER.

Dollar	1832 to 1844	$ 2,176.00
Fifty cents	1865 " 1886	383,713.00
Two reales (25 cents)	1849 " 1856	15,636.75
Twenty-five cents	1864 " 1886	121,401.75
One real	1832 " 1856	48,906.25
Half-real	1841 " 1862	15,184.93¼
Quarter-real	1845	443.18¼
Ten-cent piece	1865 " 1886	64,752.40
Five-cent piece	1865 " 1886	38,369.70

Total............$690,583.97

* Coined as experiments, and soon discontinued.

COPPER.

One-cent piece............ } 1866 to 1874 $1,681.91¼
Quarter-cent.............

RÉSUMÉ.

Gold.................................$2,351,807.875
Silver................................. 690,583.970
Copper............................... 1,681.915
                                       ──────────
    Total.......................... $3,044,073.760

VALUE OF SOME FOREIGN MONEYS IN COSTA RICA.

Pounds sterling.................. } 9 per cent. premium.
Gold of Spain.....................
Gold of France and francs....... 8¾ per cent. premium.
Gold of Colombia and Peru...... } 8¼ per cent. premium.
Gold of Mexico and Guatemala...
Gold of United States*........... 12½ per cent. premium.
Overweight onzas, each valued approximately at $17.65......... 11½ per cent. premium.

WEIGHTS AND MEASURES.

By decree of November 24, 1863, the Decimal System for moneys now in use was adopted. The people understand the system, and employ it with perfect ease; nevertheless, they retain former modes of expressing values; for example, one frequently hears: *four reals ten*, instead of 60 cents; *six reals fifteen*, instead of 90 cents.

By decree of July 10, 1884, the French Metric System was adopted for weights and measures.

──────────

* The Costarican banks will buy American gold at a premium of 50 per cent. at the present date (January, 1889). It is also greatly desired by private individuals.

WEIGHTS AND MEASURES.

AVOIRDUPOIS WEIGHT.

1 Pound — 16 ounces — 460 grams.

Quintal	Arrobas	Pounds.	Ounces.	Adarmes.	Grains.	Kilograms.
1	4	100	1,600	25,600	921,600	46.0062720
	1	25	400	6,400	230,400	11.5015680
		1	16	256	9,216	0.4600627
			1	16	576	0.0287539
				1	36	0.0017971
					1	0.0000492

APOTHECARIES WEIGHT.

Pounds.	Ounces.	Drachms.	Scruples.	Grains.	Kilograms.
1	12	96	288	6,912	0.3450470
	1	8	24	576	0.0287539
		1	3	72	0.0035942
			1	24	0.0011981
				1	0.0000449

MEASURES OF CAPACITY.—DRY MEASURE.

Fanega.	Cajuelas.	Cuartillos.	Litros.
1	24	96	899.84
	1	4	16.66
		1	4.16

The fanega is equal to nine arrobas. For coffee freights, the cart-men use a measure called carga, composed of two sacks of five arrobas each.

LIQUID MEASURE.

1 Botella (bottle) — 67 centilitros, or,
1 Litro — 1 Botella and 11.77 ounces.

OF BULLION FOR COIN.

Marco.	Onzas.	Ochavas.	Tomines.	Grains.	Kilograms.
1	8	64	384	4,608	0.23004646
....	1	8	48	576	0.02875581
....	....	1	6	72	0.00359447
....	....	....	1	12	0.00059908
....	....	....	....	1	0.00004992

LINEAL MEASURES.—VARAS (YARDS).

Vara.	Medias.	Tercias or Pies.	Cuartos or Palmeas.	Pulgadas.	Lineas.	Puntos.	Metros.
1	2	3	4	36	432	5184	0.83600
....	1	1½	2	18	216	2592	0.41800
....	....	1	1½	12	144	1728	0.27866
....	....	....	1	9	108	1296	0.20900
....	....	....	....	1	12	144	0.02322
....	....	....	....	....	1	12	0.00193
....	....	....	....	....	....	1	0.00016

MEASURES OF DISTANCE, LEAGUES OF 20,000 SPANISH FEET.

Legua.	Medias.	Kilometros.	Metros.
1	2	5	573,333
....	1	2	786,666

Legua Inglesa (Eng. League)	Milas (Miles).	Yardas.	Pies Ingleses (Eng. Feet).	Kilometros.	Metros.
1	3	5,280	15,840	4	829.42988
....	1	1,760	5,280	1	609.80996
....	....	1	3	0	0.91440
....	....	....	1	0	0.30480

The English mile, of 5,280 feet = 1,925.61 varas, or 1,609,344 metros.

LAND MEASURE.

Caballeria.	Manzanas.	Varas Cuadradas.	Hectareas.	Areas.	Metros Cuadrados or Centiareas.
1	64¼	647,500	45	25	85.16
....	1	10,000	0	69	88.96

MEASURES OF SURFACES.

Vara.	(Sq. Ft). Pies or Tercias Cuadradas.	Pulgadas Cuadradas (Sq. Inches).	Lineas Cuadrados.	Puntos Cuadrados.	Metros Cuadrados.
1	9	1,296	186,624	26,873,856	0.698896
....	1	144	20,736	2,985,984	0.077655
....	....	1	144	20,736	0.000539
....	....	....	1	144	0.000003

CUBIC MEASURE.

Vara Cubica.	Pie Cubico.	Bulgada Cubica.	Linea Cubica.	Punto Cubico.	Metros Cubicos.
1	27	46,656	80,621,568	139,314,587,904	0.584277056000
....	1	1,728	419,904	272,097,792	0.021639890962
....	......	1	1,728	2,985,984	0.000012523085
....	......	......	1	1,728	0.000000007247
....	......	......	....	1	0.000000000004

WAYS OF COMMUNICATION.

The exceptional conditions of Costa Rica appear still more interesting when the situation she occupies is considered, in relation to the points destined by nature for the uniting of the two great oceans.

On the north, the Nicaragua Canal will mark ere long her northern boundaries; on the south, the Panama route.

A simple glance at the map will show the facilities her territory affords for other interoceanic roads; either utilizing her deeper rivers in connection with wagon-ways, or by means of the railroad alone.

At present, an important mixed road crosses the central and well-settled part of the Republic, from the Pacific Port of Puntarenas to the Port of Limon on the Atlantic side.

ROAD AND TOWNS THROUGH WHICH THE PUNTARENAS-LIMON ROAD PASSES.

Puntarenas is a charming town, provided with all the traveler may desire; well supplied with excellent stores, commission houses, hotels with good service, and commodious and well-ventilated dwellings. There are some buildings worthy of attention, like the Custom House, with its spacious store-rooms; the headquarters of the Governor and the Captain of the port; also the railroad station and workshops.

The hospital fulfills its purpose satisfactorily. From 1875 to 1886 there were 570 foreigners, and 608 native patients, making in all 1,178. Of these 171 died, and 1,007 were dismissed as cured. The diseases were principally remittent fevers, dysenteries, and ulcers. It must be said that the locality is not unhealthful, but that numerous patients come from Panama.

Among private houses there are some that would do credit to towns of greater importance.

Notwithstanding the fine, long iron pier of Puntarenas, large vessels can not touch it, owing to the shallowness of water; but the launch service is excellent. On an average a thousand sacks of coffee per hour can be loaded there, by night as well as by day, if necessary.

PUNTARENAS TO SAN JOSÉ.

From Puntarenas (east) to Esparza is a distance of about fourteen miles, traversed by railroad. This is the first section of the Pacific division of the Inter-oceanic Railway. On this road the bridge constructed across the Rio Barranca is worthy of note. It is built for general traffic as well, and is one of the finest in Costa Rica. It measures 126½ yards, and is sufficiently strong for the heaviest trains of a broad-gauge road.

Esparza* is 718 feet above sea-level; a healthful place, thrifty in agriculture and business. It was named Esparza by Diego de Artieda Cherino, after his native village in Spain.

From Esparta, slightly southwest, to San Mateo, there are about twelve miles of splendid wagon-road. San Mateo is 1,050 feet above the sea, and is surrounded by fine lands for rice and other valuable productions, besides being near the principal mining center of the country. Rice has been produced in the proportion of 78 to 1; that is, from eight fanegas sown, 624 have been reaped.

---

* Changed in 1879 to Esparta.

From San Mateo (east) to Atenas, about twelve miles, the road crosses rich mineral veins, ascending the *Monte del Aguacate*, and crossing its summit at 4,132 feet altitude. The panorama presented upon these heights is one of majesty and splendor. On one side, a view of three of the principal cities of the interior, forming the center of immense cultivated tracts; on the other, virginal nature, bounded by the waters of the Gulf of Nicoya and the ocean.

Atenas is 2,379 feet above the sea. Its delightful climate, its fresh and sparkling streams, and its pleasant aspect in general, impress one most agreeably. The inhabitants are chiefly engaged in rice-growing.

From Atenas east to Garita are three miles of a very "up and down," but picturesque, road. There is also the bridge across the Rio Grande.

From Garita the wagon-road turns toward San José, passing the Llanos del Carmen (Plains of Carmen) and the Districts of San Antonio de Belen and Uruca. The distance of some twenty-one miles is traversed by a splendid wagon-road. The bridge across the Rio Virilla, with its handsome stone arches, is the most notable work in this locality.

The wagon-road divides at Garita, one part turning off northeast toward Alajuela. This part measures nine miles, is very level, and with more frequent habitations than thus far.

In Alajuela, at an elevation of 3,001 feet, begins the central division of the railway. This division measures twenty-six and one-half miles, and terminates in Cartago, as follows:

```
Alajuela to Heredia ................... 7   miles.
Heredia (3,786 feet high) to San José...... 6¼    "
San José (3,868 feet high) to Tres Rios.... 6¼    "
Tres Rios (attaining an elevation of 5,265
    feet en route) to Cartago (4,930 feet)..... 7  "
```

The railroad connects many smaller towns.

On this route there are many fine bridges. The Virilla bridge measures 109 feet, and is built 100 feet above the water; the Padre Hidalgo is 133 feet long and 50 high; the Quebrada del Fierro is 185 feet long and 60 high. These bridges are iron, resting on bulwarks of solid masonry.

To repeat, from Puntarenas to San José, sixty-two miles, thirty-six miles of which, between Alajuela and Esparza, may be traveled in ten hours with good horses, which can be secured in either town at moderate prices.

The hotels of Esparza, San Mateo, Atenas, and Alajuela are comfortable, and the service good.

FROM SAN JOSÉ TO PORT LIMON.

From San José to Carrillo, a distance of twenty-five miles, is a remarkably good wagon-road, which may be traveled in six hours, as follows:

San José (3,868 feet high) to San Vicente... 8 miles.
San Vicente (4,098 feet high) to Rio Macho. 8 "
Rio Macho (4,276 feet high) to San Jeronimo 1½ "
San Jeronimo (4,490 feet high) to La Palma 8 "
La Palma (5,000 feet high) to La Hondura.. 3 "
La Hondura (3,900 feet high) to La Laguna 2½ "
La Laguna (3,300 feet high) to Boca del Infierno .... 3 "
Boca del Infierno (2,398 feet high) to Carrillo 6 "
Carrillo, by railroad, to Limon............70

The railroad has eight principal bridges on this division; those of—

Rio Sucio........................	440	feet.
" Toro Amarillo..................	505	"
" Reventazon	268	"
" Pacuare......................	255	"
" Camarones....................	206	"
" Madre de Dios.................	280	"
" Matina........................	1,489	"
" Estero de Moin................	400	"

There are also twenty-two of from 100 to 200 and 250 under 100 feet.

Another notable work is the construction of the road for four and one-half miles across a marsh, for which purpose stone and earth had to be brought in great quantities from a long distance.

The pretty Port of Limon is the principal entrance from the sea of the Antilles and the great North. The town of Limon, though but a few years old, is reasonably advanced, and one can live there with comfort and safety, although fevers are inevitable unless the strictest regularity of living be observed. There are good houses, hotels, stores, and commission offices.

The Limon pier is 655 feet long by 35 broad,

At Limon.

with an extension of 250 by 50 feet at its head. When vessels touch at the pier, the freight is loaded directly from cars to steamer, or *vice versa*. Over 1,800 bunches of bananas have thus been loaded aboard a steamer in less than twelve hours.

The two drawbacks of the port have thus far been the bad drinking water and the existence of stagnant marshes in the near vicinity, evils which it is hoped may soon be remedied.

A hospital and quarantine buildings are in construction on the Island of Uvita, close by.

Work on the railway branch between Cartago and Reventazon is now being rapidly pushed ahead; this done, one can travel all the way from Alajuela to Port Limon by rail.

A year or two since a smaller port was opened at the mouth of the Rio Colorado, on the Atlantic, and navigation established thence to the San Juan, as an easy means of communication with the Sarapaqui and San Carlos Rivers, natural arteries for future commerce of the Heredia and Alajuela Provinces. Two small vessels are devoted to this purpose. The question of roads to these rivers has been considered at various times; that for the Sarapaqui was carried out in the fifties to the extent of some leagues of wagon-way. The enterprise was abandoned from the time of the Walker war, and little thought given it until the past year or so, when the Government undertook the work of completing it.

Another inter-oceanic route presents itself, of easy construction, according to all reports, utilizing the San Carlos River, and opening communication with the Pacific by rail or wagon-road to Puntarenas, benefiting thereby a vast extent of splendid territory.

Various other localities present facilities for inter-oceanic routes; the day may not be distant when a railroad will cross the Isthmus from Bocas del Toro to Golfo Dulce, or elsewhere in the Pacific.

All the towns or villages of Costa Rica are connected by wagon-roads more or less well built, excepting the City of Liberia, in the Province of Guanacaste, communication with which is effected by Puntarenas and the Gulf of Nicoya, for the reason that this way is a convenient one, and also that in the rainy season the tract between Esparza and Bagaces can not be traveled, by reason of its dangerous rivers. The navigation of the Gulf of Nicoya is chiefly that of little steamers carrying the Guanacaste mail.

Communication with the extreme south coast is made with small boats carrying the mails to Terraba and Boruca, at the north of Golfo Dulce.

Various new roads are being built, like that from San Ramon to Nicaragua; that of Santa Maria to Paquita; and that leading to the lowlands of General, where a live-stock farm is to be established.

By a contract with the Government, a company is now engaged in canalization of the rivers and tributaries between the San Juan and Matina, for the navigation of suitable vessels. Thus equipped, that vast region of land will be developed in the line of cocoanuts, valuable woods, and other articles.

MAILS.

Since 1873 the mail service has been considerably improved. Of late the Republic has joined the Universal Postal Union, greatly to its own advantage.

The improvement in the service may be judged from the comparison of the three years given:

In 1811 were dispatched............... 600 cartas.
In 1874 were dispatched............... 32,500 cartas.
In 1888, general movement.............

Correspondence for foreign countries is dispatched by steamers touching at Puntarenas and Port Limon, itineraries being arranged permitting one to write five times per month. The frequent arrivals of banana steamers in Limon increase the facilities. Nearly every month extra mails are thus dispatched to Europe and the United States.

The domestic mail service is well arranged, and highly acceptable.

Although the dispatching of mails is constantly subject to change, according to the itineraries of steamers and railroads, a table is given below from which one may gain an idea of the arrivals and departures of mails:

ITINERARY OF MAILS—MONTH OF APRIL, 1889.

Domestic.	Departure—Days.	Hour.	Arrival—Days.
Liberia, Santa Cruz, and Nicoya	Mon., Wed., and Fri.	4 p. m.	Mon. and Thur.
Puntarenas and road	Daily.	4 p. m.	Daily.
Cartago, Alajuela, Heredia, San Joaquin, Union, and San Domingo	Twice daily.	10 a. m. and	Twice daily.
Carrillo and Limon	Daily.	4 p. m.	Daily.
Alajuelita, San Sebastian, and Hatilo	Mon. and Fri.	10 a. m	Mon. and Fri.
Aserri, Desamparados, Mojon, and Curridabat	Mon. and Thur.	10 a. m.	Mon. and Fri.
San Vicente, Guadalupe, San Juan, and San Isidro	Tues. and Thur.	10 a. m.	Tues. and Thur.
Le Uruca and San Antonio de Belen	Wed.	10 a. m.	Wed.
Puriscal, Mora, Santa Ana, and Escasu	Mon. and Thur.	7 a. m.	Wed. and Sat.
Sarapiqui and San Carlos	Saturday, April 6.	4 p. m.	Uncertain.
San Carlos, via Naranjo	Sat.	4 p.m.	Sat.
Desamparados and Escasu	Mon. to Sat.	8 a. m.	Mon. to Sat.
Golfo Dulce	Thursday, April 11.	4 p. m.	Uncertain.
Paraiso	Daily.	4 p. m.	Daily.
Orosi and Juan Viñas	Mon., Wed., and Fri.	10 a. m.	Mon., Wed., and Fri.
Talamanca	The 12th and 26th.	4 p. m.	Uncertain.
San Ignacio de Aserri, Guatil, and road	Thur.	8 p. m.	Thur.
Tarrazu	Thur.	4 p. m.	Thur.
Heredia to San Isidro	Tues. and Fri.	6 p. m.	Tues. and Fri.

MAILS.

Heredia to Barba and Santa Barbara	Daily.	6 p. m.	Daily.	
Alajuela to Grecia	Daily.	1 p. m.	Daily.	
Grecia to Naranjo and road	Daily.	....	Daily.	
San Antonio de Belen, via Heredia	Daily.	4 p. m.	Daily.	
Heredia to San Rafael	Daily.	6 p. m.	Daily.	
De Alajuela to San Pedro and Sabanilla	Tues., Thur., and Sat.	12 m.	Tues., Thur., and Sat.	

FOREIGN.

Europe, United States, Antilles and South America, via Puntarenas and Panama	8, 9, 18, and 26.	4 p. m.	2, 8, 18, and 22.
Via Limon and Colon	15.	4 p. m.	14.
California and Mexico	30.	4 p. m.	17.
Nicaragua, Honduras, Salvador, and Guatemala	11, 20, and 30.	4 p. m.	10, 11, 20, and 28.
Nicaragua, via Liberia	Wed.	4 p. m.	Thur.
Europe and United States, via Limon	Fri.	4 p. m.	Uncertain.
Europe, by Hamburg line	1st.	....	3rd.

TELEGRAPH.

Costa Rica was the first Central American republic to have the telegraph. The first steps toward it were taken in 1857, and further attention given it in 1866; but it was 1869 when the first line was completed from Puntarenas to Cartago. Since then it has been extended in all directions. There are 389 miles of wire, and offices as follows:

Alajuela,	Guasimal,	Paraiso,
Ascrri,	Heredia,	Puntarenas,
Atenas,	Jimenez,	Puriscal,
Bagaces,	La Barranca,	San José,
Barba,	La Cruz,	San Mateo,
Bebedero,	La Palma,	San Rafael,
Carrillo,	La Union,	San Ramon,
Cartago,	Liberia,	Santa Barbara,
Desamparados,	Limon,	Santo Domingo,
Escasu,	Matina,	Siquirres.
Esparza,	Naranjo,	
Grecia,	Pacaca,	

Communication with all Central America is considered the same as within the country. The price for ten words is 20 cents, and for every five or less additional, 5 cents.

Eleven of the offices mentioned have been opened, and more than fifty miles of wire strung, under the direction of Don F. Roberto Castro, during the Soto administration.

The railroad has a special wire from Cartago to Alajuela, which is not included in the above figures.

CABLE.

The office of the Cable Company is at San Juan del Sur, Nicaragua, not far from the

Costarican line. The Government is making efforts to secure an office within its own territory.

CABLE TARIFF—PER WORD—JANUARY, 1889.

Costarican Money.

United States—except Texas, Louisiana and Key West	$1.58
United States—Texas (except Galveston and Louisiana)	1.46
United States—Galveston	1.39
United States—Key West	1.58
Great Britain, France and Germany	1.93
Belgium	2.03
Italy	2.08
Spain	2.19
Holland	2.06
Ecuador—Guayaquil and Santa Elena	1.18
Peru—Payta	1.46
Peru—Callao and Lima	1.74
Cuba	2.36
Chili	3.42
Mexico—Vera Cruz, Tehuantepec, etc	.45
Mexico City	.54

UNITED STATES OF COLOMBIA.

Panama	.34
Colon	.41
Buenaventura	.79

TELEPHONE.

Service was established in 1886 in San José.

POLITICAL INSTITUTIONS.

The Government is popular, representative, alternative, and responsible.

There are three distinct authorities: Legislative, Executive, and Judicial.

The Legislative is exercised by representatives of the people, the body being called the Constitutional Congress.

The suffrage is of two grades. The elections are conducted as follows: Popular conventions are held to elect a limited number of electors; these latter meet in a body called the Electoral Assembly, and proceed to elect the President of the Republic, the Congressmen, or Municipals, as the case may be.*

The Executive authority is vested in the President of the Republic, who has the power of naming and removing the Secretaries of State. The President is elected as is the Congress.

The Judicial authority is vested in the Supreme Court of Justice and in the Tribunals and Judicatures under it established by law.

The three are changed every four years. The President is not eligible to immediate re-election.

PUBLIC ADMINISTRATION.

The Republic is divided into five provinces and two comarcas, and these into cantons subdivided into districts.

---

*"In the popular conventions there may take part any Costarican, native of the Republic or naturalized, who lives by his labor, has completed his twenty-first year, or his eighteenth should he be married or professor of a science, and who enjoys citizenship.

"To be a member of the Electoral Assembly, it is necessary that one, besides being twenty-one years of age, should know how to read and write, be a resident of the Province the popular convention corresponding to which has named him, and possess a fortune of not less than $500 or an annual income of $200."—*Ricardo Jimenez, Instruccion Civica.*

Each canton has a municipality popularly elected, and a Political Chief named by the President.

In each of the provinces and comarcas there is a Governor and a Commandant of Arms, also named by the President, and a Judge of the First Instance, appointed by the Supreme Court.

RIGHTS AND PRIVILEGES.

Respect for creeds, home, and property is observed. There has never been infringement of these rights in Costa Rica, nor retroactive laws framed. If private property is required for public purposes, there is always just indemnification.

The sacredness of correspondence, the right to meet in bodies and to petition, the right of *habeas corpus*, the liberty of the press, all are guaranteed by the Constitution.

The suspension of individual privileges can only be ordered by the Constitutional Congress, or its Permanent Commission in exceptional cases.

Foreigners enjoy all civil rights without being admitted to citizenship or being compelled to contribute heavy sums. Admission to citizenship may be asked for at any time, and will be granted, as in most civilized countries, after one year's residence.

RELIGION.

Under the Colonial rule, and for some years

after, this country was subject in the matter of ecclesiastical government to the Episcopate of Leon of Nicaragua, established soon after the Conquest.

After the Independence the religious spirit did not decline.

The first constitutive law of the Province, provisional in character, put forth in December, 1821, had as follows:

"Article 3. The religion of the Province is and shall be always the Catholic, Apostolic, Roman, as the only true one, exclusive of any other.

"Article 4. If any stranger of different religion shall arrive in this Province in the pursuit of business or travel, the Government shall assign to him the precise time that he shall remain, during which time he shall be protected as to liberty and security of person and property, always provided he shall not engage in sedition against Church or State, in which case he shall be immediately expelled."

Such restrictions were natural, considering the spirit of the age and the preponderance of the clergy, and notwithstanding the fact that there were many illustrious citizens who gave proofs of more liberal spirit in the organization of the Province.

The first definitive Constitution, issued January 21, 1825, guaranteed by its Article 2 liberty of thought, speech, and pen. But in Article 25 it declared as the official religion the Catholic, Apostolic, Roman, which it should protect with wise laws; and by decree of September 23, of the same year, penalties were established, regarding as infraction of the law any irreverence or lack of respect toward the religion of the country.

Religious freedom advanced considerably from the year 1842, not only as to laws, but as to tolerance in all classes of society. In that year cemeteries were provided for non-Catholics, and in 1847 a Protestant congregation was in existence. The present tolerance for other beliefs is obvious in the fact that the one church in all Central America consecrated to a religion different from that of the country, stands to-day in San José of Costa Rica, not more than 125 yards from the great Catholic Cathedral.

On the 28th of April, 1870, a law of privileges declared freedom of thought to be absolute.

The Constitution in force only establishes tolerance, but deep in the hearts of all Costaricans are implanted the principles of liberty in matters of conscience, in which each one should be guided by his own idea of right.

The great majority of Costaricans being of Catholic, Roman, and Apostolic faith, the Government protects that religion, and contributes to its support with sums from the National Treasury.

The onerous exaction of the *diezmo* contribution suffered the first blows under the administration of Benemerito Don Juan Mora Fernandez.

From the year 1825, when Guanacaste was at last firmly annexed, the Costarican live-stock owners of that district worked hard to have this tax abolished, but without success. Nor did the Bishopric of Costa Rica, decreed September 29, 1825, succeed. It was opposed by the Bishop of Nicaragua, as contrary to his temporal interests.

The *diezmos* were suppressed at length, and in 1835 many of the feast days were done away with, as also processions outside of the churches upon working days.

In 1847 Dr. Don José M. Castro came into office; he opened communication with Rome, and procured the establishment of a Bishopric in Costa Rica. On April 10, 1851, Rev. Anselmo Llorente y La Fuente was made Bishop, and consecrated in Guatemala, September 7th, of the same year. The first Dean and Vicar was the Rev. Rafael del Carmen Calvo.

Although the *diezmo* tax had been reëstablished in 1836, the people of the country fought against it, and it was abolished forever by President Mora's energetic opposition to Bishop Llorente.

The Government formed a covenant at that time with the Holy See, which was maintained until 1885, when it was declared inconvenient for the Nation.

PUBLIC INSTRUCTION.

The first steps toward the organization of educational institutions were taken under the administration of Don Juan Mora Fernandez; in this period public instruction became of importance, and it was declared obligatory upon the State to propagate it. The institution which afterward became the University of Santo Tomas was founded in 1844, at the instance of Doctor Castro, an institution which has been the *alma mater* of many of the country's notable men.

The efforts have been great and sustained to advance education, and it is to be remarked that those in office have constantly shown laudable interest in the matter.

In 1869 the Normal School was opened, and a system adopted in harmony with modern ideas.

The Constitution provides that: "Elementary instruction of both sexes is obligatory, free, and provided for by the Government. The immediate supervision shall be for the Municipality; the supreme inspection for the Executive. . . . . Every Costarican or foreigner is free to give or receive instruction in institutions which are not maintained at public expense."

The number of schools for elementary instruction maintained by the Government in Costa Rica in 1886 was 260, with an attendance of about 20,000 pupils of both sexes. In addition there were 96 private schools, with an attendance of 3,000 pupils.

For higher education there are three colleges: The San José University, the San Luis College, in Cartago, and the San Agustin College, in Heredia.

There is a young ladies' school in San José and one in Alajuela.

In San José there is the University of Santo Tomas, with established professorships for various courses.

The Normal and Model Schools, established in 1886, do honor to Central America. To the hard work and energy of the Minister of Public Instruction, Don Mauro Fernandez, many of the best results are attributed.

According to the census of 1883, 12 per cent. of the inhabitants know how to read and write, and 14 per cent. to read only. The idea is obtaining that not a single Costarican but should receive the benefits of education. To this end the Government is directing its strongest efforts.

The following tables show the territorial educational divisions of Costa Rica by cantons and districts:

PUBLIC INSTRUCTION.

PROVINCE OF SAN JOSÉ.

FIRST CANTON—SAN JOSÉ.

School Districts.

I. San José (city).
II. Guadalupe.
III. San Isidro.
IV. San Juan.
V. San Vicente.
VI. Alajuelita.
VII. Curridabat.
VIII. La Uruca.
IX. San Sebastian.
X. El Zapote.
XI. San Pedro.
XII. Sabanilla.
XIII. San Jeronimo.
XIV. Las Pavas.
XV. Dos Rios.
XVI. Hatillo.
XVII. Mata Redondo.

SECOND CANTON—PURISCAL.

School Districts.

I. Santiago (village).
II. San Rafael.
III. San Pablo.
IV. San Antonio.
V. Candelaria.
VI. Desamparaditos.

THIRD CANTON—ASERRI.

School Districts.

I. Aserri (village).
II. San Ignacio.
III. Guaytil.

FOURTH CANTON—DESAMPARADOS.

School Districts.

I. Desamparados (village).
II. San Miguel.
III. San Rafael.
IV. San Juan de Dios.
V. Patarra.
VI. San Cristobal.
VII. El Rosario.

FIFTH CANTON—ESCASU.

School Districts.

I. Escasu (village).
II. Santa Ana.
III. Uruca.

SIXTH CANTON—PACACA.

School Districts.

I. Pacaca (village).
II. Tabarcia.
III. Guayabo.

SEVENTH CANTON—TARRAZU.

School Districts.

I. Santa Maria.
II. San Marcos.

PROVINCE OF ALAJUELA.

FIRST CANTON—ALAJUELA.

School Districts.

I. Alajuela (city).
II. San Pedro.
III. Sabanvilla.
IV. San Rafael.
V. San José.
VI. San Antonio.
VII. Santiago del Este.
VIII. Concepcion.
IX. Desamparados.
X. San Isidro.
XI. Carrillos.

SECOND CANTON—GRECIA.

School Districts.

I. Grecia (village).
II. San Jeronimo.
III. Santa Gertrudis.
IV. Sarchi—South.
V. Sarchi—North.
VI. Los Angeles.
VII. Tacares.
VIII. Puente de Piedra.

PROVINCE OF ALAJUELA.—CONTINUED.

THIRD CANTON—SAN RAMON.
School Districts.
I. San Ramon (village).
II. Palmares.
III. Santiago.
IV. San Rafael.
V. Concepcion.
VI. Piedades—South.
VII. Piedades—North.
VIII. San Juan.

FOURTH CANTON—NARANJO.
School Districts.
I. Naranjo (village).
II. San Juanillo.

III. San Miguel.
IV. Candelaria.
V. Barranca.
VI. Palmitos.
VII. Zarcero.

FIFTH CANTON—ATENAS.
School Districts.
I. Atenas (village).
II. Jesus.

SIXTH CANTON—SAN MATEO.
School Districts.
I. San Mateo (village).
II. Santo Domingo.

PROVINCE OF CARTAGO.

FIRST CANTON—CARTAGO.
School Districts.
I. Cartago (city).
II. San Rafael.
III. San Nicolas.
IV. Angeles.
V. Concepcion.
VI. El Carmen.
VII. Guadalupe.
VIII. El Hervidero.
IX. Los Cipreses.
X. San Juan de Tobosi.
XI. El Llano.
XII. Las Pacayas.
XIII. Cot.
XIV. Tobosi.

XV. Cervantes.
XVI. Santa Cruz.

SECOND CANTON—PARAISO.
School Districts.
I. Paraiso (village).
II. Turrialba.
III. Juan Viñas.
IV. Cachi.
V. Orosi.

THIRD CANTON—LA UNION.
School Districts.
I. La Union (village).
II. Concepcion.
III. San Diego.

PROVINCE OF HEREDIA.

FIRST CANTON—HEREDIA.
School Districts.
I. Heredia (city).
II. San Isidro.
III. San Pablo.
IV. Mercedes.
V. San Francisco.
VI. Barreal.
VII. San Joaquin.

VIII. La Rivera.
IX. San Antonio.

SECOND CANTON—SANTO DOMINGO.
School Districts.
I. Santo Domingo (village).
II. Santo Tomas.
III. Santa Rosa.
IV. San Miguel.

PUBLIC INSTRUCTION.

PROVINCE OF HEREDIA.—CONTINUED.

THIRD CANTON—SAN RAFAEL.
School Districts.
I. San Rafael (village).
II. Centro Sur-oeste.
III. Los Angeles.

FOURTH CANTON—BARBA.
School Districts.
I. Barba (village).
II. San Pedro.

FIFTH CANTON—SANTA BARBARA.
School Districts.
I. Santa Barbara (village).
II. San Juan.
III. Jesus.

PROVINCE OF GUANACASTE.

FIRST CANTON—LIBERIA.
School Districts.
I. Liberia (city).
II. Sardinal.
III. Boquerones.

SECOND CANTON—SANTA CRUZ.
School Districts.
I. Santa Cruz (village).
II. Belen.
III. Veintisiete de Abril (April 26th).
IV. Santa Barbara.
V. Tempate.

THIRD CANTON—NICOYA.
School Districts.
I. Nicoya (village).
II. San Rafael.
III. Santa Rita.
IV. Corralillo.
V. Pueblo Viejo.
VI. Matambu.

FOURTH CANTON—CANAS.
School Districts.
I. Cañas (village).

FIFTH CANTON—BAJACES.
School Districts.
I. Bajaces (village).

COMARCAS.

PUNTARENAS.

FIRST CANTON—PUNTARENAS.
School Districts.
I. Puntarenas (city).
II. Golfo Dulce.

SECOND CANTON—ESPARTA.
School District.
I. Esparta (city).

LIMON.

ONLY CANTON—LIMON.
School District.
I. Limon (city).

LEGISLATION AND COURTS.

Costa Rica was the first of the Central American Republics to effect complete emancipation from the Spanish and Colonial laws, and one of the first countries of Spanish America to provide herself with laws in harmony with a new mode of political being and with the progress of civilization.

In 1841, under the administration of Don Braulio Carrillo, there went into effect the first edition of the General Code, including the Civil, Penal, and Code of Proceedings, which, with some important reforms introduced in the second edition, 1858, is still in force.

The works upon Legislation, especially since the establishment of the College of Lawyers, have been incessant and powerful.

In the Penal Code, in effect since 1880, the death penalty is abolished, as well as other humiliating and cruel punishments; and in 1886 there was promulgated a new Civil Code, in which are prominent, as triumphs of the present administration, the civil marriage, divorce, and civil liberty of woman.

The Code of Commerce in force, founded on the Spanish, was issued in 1853.

The Fiscal Code of to-day went into effect in 1885.

The Military Code of 1871 was superseded in 1884 by another more in harmony with modern institutions.

Don Maximo Fernandez, Judge of Supreme Court.

The Jury System in criminal cases has existed since 1873.

The Municipal Statutes in force to-day were issued in 1867; the General Police Regulations in 1849.

The "Ley Organica" Law of Tribunals was framed in 1845, and modified slightly in 1852.

In 1865, there was promulgated the law for Creditors' Proceedings, which has proved a good one.

Higher and professional education was provided for in 1843, by a law known as the Statutes of the University of Santo Tomas, and in 1886 there was given a law for common education.

The Mortgage Law was passed in 1865.

There are, besides, many special laws, like the Mining Statutes, decreed in 1830; the Water Law of 1884, now in force; the Consular Regulations of recent passing, and others.

The Supreme Court of Justice is formed of the Court of Law, with five Magistrates, and two Boards of the Second Instance, with three Magistrates each.

In each of the provinces and the Comarca of Puntarenas, there are Judges of Criminal and Civil Proceedings.

In the head towns of each Canton, the Alcaldes act in civil cases of less importance, and in criminal cases are Judges of lesser offenses, who take evidence concerning the graver.

In the districts, the Justices of the Peace, as Police, are charged with the public order, and act in ordinary matters.

For fiscal affairs, there are an Inspector General of Hacienda, an Alcalde of Hacienda, and a National Judge of Hacienda.

There is also a special Judge of Mines residing at San Mateo.

PENALTIES.

The punishments are generally neither cruel nor extended. They are arrest, confinement in prison or penitentiary, transportation, or fine. The penitentiary is on the Island of San Lucas.

The disagreeable spectacle of prisoners dragging their chains and balls through the streets is now never seen.

PROPERTY REGISTRATION.

The property owners are so numerous, and the Costarican's habits of order so marked, this being an essentially agricultural country, that the necessity of a mortgage law was apparent, for the purpose of maintaining and securing the rights of all.

The Registry of Property and Mortgages was opened in 1867, since when various reforms have been introduced in the mortgage law.

NATIONAL REVENUES.

The progress in financial affairs may be seen from the following tables:

NATIONAL REVENUES.

CONDITION OF THE NATIONAL TREASURY FOR THE MONTHS FROM JANUARY TO SEPTEMBER, 1824.

AMOUNTS RECEIVED.

Tribunal of Commerce Branch.	$ 819—7½ [reals]	
Returns—C. Rafael Gallegos...	31—7	
From Tobacco Factory........	9,655—4¼	$10,007—3

DEPOSITS.

Redemption of Captives........	$ 131—3¼	
Aguardiente Branch............	3,430—1	
Customs.......................	391—1	
Stamped Paper.................	351—6	
Quinto Tax....................	440—0	4,744—3¼
Total.........................		$14,243—7¼

AMOUNTS PAID OUT.

Balance made up by the Minister the year previous............................	$ 77—6¼
Salary of Supreme Government..........	1,403—4
Captain and Soldiers of the Port of the South...............................	538—1
Parish Priests.........................	131—1
Various Payments into other Treasuries..	335—6
To Widows and Orphans................	340—0
To Veterans, balances of 1821, 1823, and 1824.................................	3,311—5
To Militia and Artillery of 1823.........	6,145—4
Relief for Soldiers of Matina............	239—0
Receipts for Consolidation.............	83—6
General Expenses (33 divisions).........	1,135—7
Expenses Extraordinary................	96—7
Salary of Minister.....................	405—0
Total.................................	$14,243—7¼

DEMONSTRATION.

Amounts received.....................	$14,751—6¼
" paid out.....................	14,243—7¼
Balance in Treasury...................	507—7 rs.

[Signed] MANUEL GARCIA ESCALANTE.

San José, Sept. 30, 1824.

In 1840 the tax receipts were $117,164.3
The expenses amounted to 67,992.6¼
The customs produced $29,696—6 reals that year.

In 1860 the receipts were $645,550.2¼
And the amounts paid out............... 588,602.6¼

From 1879 to 1880 the taxes produced ..$2,525,726.12
And the expenses were................. 3,158,823.72
Deficit of............................. 638,097.60

For the economic year of 1885 to 1886 the
revenue produced $3,200,064.57
And the expenditure was 3,088,944.28

The present revenue is composed of Custom House duties; revenue stamps and stamped paper; liquor and tobacco monopolies; sale of public lands; tax for registering property and on slaughtering of live-stock; products of railroads, telegraph, postal service, and other property.

For the economic year of 1888 to 1889 the following figures are given:

Revenue $3,639,856.90
Miscellaneous and extraordinary receipts 505,725.96

Total..........................$4,145,582.86
Expenditure........................ 3,939,997.75

At present the income of the Treasury is composed of—custom duties; sale of stamped and official paper; liquor and tobacco monopolies; sale of unappropriated lands; registration fees; liquor rights; results of railroads, telegraph, mail, and other National properties.

As is seen, there are no direct contributions.

In the economic year of 1885–86 the income was as follows:

NATIONAL DEBT—FOREIGN DEBT.

Customs	$ 867,263.88
Liquor Monopolies	747,960.78
Tobacco Monopolies	466,973.86
Railroad	112,759.83
Other Receipts	1,005,106.22
Total	$3,200,064.57

The expenses of the Administration for the same year were:

Appropriation for Government	$ 231,928.47
Appropriation for Police	82,979.80
Appropriation for Justice	68,360.68
Appropriation for Patronage	194,750.27
Appropriation for War, including part of cost of appurtenances lately purchased	359,504.25
Appropriation for Public Instruction	93,320.61
Appropriation for Foreign Relations	39,267.65
Appropriation for Religious Affairs	15,324.33
Appropriation for Marine Affairs	17,667.27
Appropriation for Charitable Affairs	2,377.10
Appropriation for Hacienda	154,712.41
Domestic Debt, etc	502,592.41
Exploitation of Monopolies	294,085.12
Costa Rica Railway	166,731.72
Various Expenses	865,342.19
Total	$3,088,944.28

NATIONAL DEBT

Is as follows:

Foreign debt, converted at 5 per cent. (£2,000,000)	$10,000,000
Interior debt, converted at 12 per cent	872,093
Paper of the country in circulation	1,069,983
Total	$11,942,076

FOREIGN DEBT.

In October, 1885, the exterior debt amounted to £4,810,812, as the result of unfortunate investments of 1871-72. This sum, at legal rate of exchange, amounted to $26,218,425.40, of which it appears Costa Rica received only

$4,877,865.56, and found it necessary to establish proceedings in London against the bankers who took part in the disastrous negotiation.

The efforts of the Government, sustained at considerable expense, did not effect the hoped-for results. However, a special arrangement was effected with Mr. Minor C. Keith, the well-known manager of the Costa Rica Railway, by which the liquidation of the debt might be managed, through the construction of a branch required to connect the Atlantic division with that terminating in Cartago. As a result of this negotiation the exterior debt was reduced to (£2,000,000) $10,000,000, the interest of which at 5 per cent. and mortmain at 1 per cent. per annum should be paid in advance in 1888, from the Custom House receipts, and a railway company (with a capital of $6,000,000, Costarican money) was organized, the Nation not sharing responsibility. The railway company was conceded the lease of the road, from Limon to Alajuela, for the period of ninety-nine years, the Government taking a third of the shares and receiving a third of the dividends of the enterprise, and reserving the right to make use of it. The company receives, besides, 400,000 acres of unappropriated National lands, in the products of or realization upon which the Government shall have interest. This company receives, besides, 400,000 acres of public lands, of the realization or products of which the Government may retain one-third.

On January 1, 1888, the payment of the last interest coupon was effected in London, and July 1st of the same year the first was paid, on direct account of the Government of Costa Rica. January 1, 1889, the second was paid, and July 1st the third, amounting to £50,000 each.

The efforts of the Government to maintain and protect the public credit have resulted in the rise of Costarican consolidated paper in London, so that in May, 1889, bonds of Series A were quoted at 94 to 95, and those of Series B at 92½ to 93½.

INTERIOR DEBT.

The interior debt, converted at 12 per cent., November 30, 1882, amounted to $1,594,483.96. From that date the mortmain has been verified, applying each year the income from customs, in such a way that it has been reduced to $870,244.75.

NATIONAL BILLS.

The confidence of the public in this mode of circulation permits the Government to invest the mortmain of its paper under the best conditions, since it circulates as actual money; nevertheless, a sum is appropriated for the payment of the notes, should this become necessary.

INTERNATIONAL RELATIONS.

At all times the Government has displayed wisdom and circumspection in its relations with foreign countries. The Republic has maintained its traditional policy of non-interference in the affairs of its neighbors; and may even congratulate itself upon having, at different times, exercised a good influence upon its sister countries of Central America.

Costa Rica has, in various countries, accredited legations of the first order; also consular representatives in many of the cities in the countries with which she holds official relations.

There are likewise accredited to the Republic, although with residence in Guatemala, the Legations of Germany, France, Great Britain, Spain, Italy, United States of America, Mexico, Ecuador, etc.; and there are resident in Costa Rica, consular agents of the countries named, and of many others of Europe and America.

ARMY.

All Costaricans between eighteen and fifty years of age are obliged to do military service according to law.

The army is divided in two parts: The first includes, under the head of active service, all soldiers from eighteen to forty years of age; the second includes all the rest, under the head of "Reserve."

There is a third division, known as the

National Guard, including all citizens capable of shouldering arms outside of the foregoing.

The permanent force can be raised to 1,000 men, ordinarily; in times of interior commotion, to 5,000; and in the event of war with other countries to whatever number is required.

PRINTING, NEWSPAPERS, AND PUBLISHERS.

The epoch of Central American Independence arrived without printing being known in Costa Rica.

In Guatemala, notwithstanding the importance given to that Kingdom since 1543, and printing being known from 1660, it was not until the beginning of the 18th century that the first paper was published, called *La Gaceta Mensual* (the Monthly Gazette).

La Sociedad Economica was the second paper published in the Kingdom. The Economic Society of Friends, founded in 1795, in Guatemala, by Don Jacob de Villaurrutia, had as its object the advancement of art, industry, agriculture, and education in general; in order to promote its ideas, it began, in 1815, to issue the sheet of that name.

In spite of the despotism of Colonial authorities, there was circulated in Guatemala, in 1820, the *Editor Constitucional* and the *Amigo de la Patria*. A third followed in 1821, *El Genio de la Libertad*.

In 1824, the *Semanario Politico Mercantil*

appeared in Salvador; three years later the first paper of this Republic; in 1830 the first paper in Honduras, *La Gaceta*, and the same year the first one in Nicaragua.

Costa Rica meanwhile followed the old system of making known by proclamation the gubernatorial decrees; public opinion had no other medium of expression than by speech in social gatherings or at meetings convoked by the authorities.

A little before Independence, some manuscripts were circulated bearing upon the direction of opinions, and even during the government of Don Juan Mora the founding of a paper was considered, which should make public the requirements of the people. The lack of presses being felt, efforts were at once made to provide the same, and, in 1830, the decrees of the Government first appeared in type. This press* was imported by Don Miguel Carranza.

The first newspaper of Costa Rica was published in 1832, by Don Joaquin Bernardo Calvo. It was called *El Noticioso Universal*, and it was followed a year later by *La Tertulia*, an opposition organ.

Until the year 1883, there were only six presses throughout the country, and scarcely more than forty-six printers.

Costa Rica has had, nevertheless, many

---

* It is now to be seen in the San José Museum.

papers worthy of mention—the *Mentor Costarricense*, the *Guerrillero*, the *Eco de Irazu*, *La Cronica*, *La Epoca*, *El Costarricense*, *El Travieso*, etc.

Later came *La Patria*, edited by Don Manuel Felipe Quiros, Don Angel A. Castro, and Don Maximo Fernandez.

The newspapers published at present are: *El Diario*, *Costarricense*, *La Republica*, and *La Gaceta* (official).

There are, also: *El Maestro*, scientific; *La Enseñanza*, monthly educational review; *El Foro*, organ of the Lawyers' College. There are ten presses in the Republic, seven being at San José, and about 100 printers.

The Imprenta Nacional is an important establishment, where sometimes five presses are running at the same time, by steam-power.

Other kinds of publications have not been lacking. Text-books for the schools, edited by Don R. F. Osejo, Don Joaquin Gonzalez, Don Tadeo Gomez, Don Alfonso Cinelli, Don A. M. Velasquez, Don C. F. Salazar, Don E. Villavicencio, Don Francisco M. Barrantes, and Don Ricardo Jimenez.

The Doctors Don Salvador Jimenez and Don Rafael Orozco have written works upon the Civil and Penal Laws of National interest.

The three first volumes of documents toward a history of Costa Rica have been edited, and the same published by Don Leon Fernandez.

Every year a volume of laws enacted in the country is published. The *Anuario Estadistico* (Annual Statistician), the *Ministerial Memorials*, etc., etc., are also issued.

DISTINGUISHED MEN.

Among those born in Costa Rica are the following: The Rev. Father José de Liendo y Goicoechea, learned in Experimental Philosophy, and who was persecuted in Spain by the Inquisition, and who became one of the editors of the *Gaceta del Reino* of Guatemala. The Señor Don José Maria Zamora y Coronado, who came of an old Cartago family, was born in 1785, occupied high posts in Cuba, became Regent of the Audiencia Pretorial of Havana, and still later filled higher offices. His *Biblioteca de Legislacion Ultramarina* alone should suffice to make his name familiar to posterity. Another notable Costarican was Dr. Don Florencio de Castillo, who distinguished himself in the celebrated Court of Cadiz of 1812.

Of later times: The Rev. Dr. Don Juan de los Santos Madriz, member of the Upper Gubernatorial Council, and Delegate to various political assemblies during the years 1821–1824, was noted for his efforts to advance education. The Licenciate Don Agustin Gutierrez Lizaurzabal, first jurisconsulate in Costa Rica, and President of the first State Legislative Assembly. The Licenciate Don Braulio Carrillo, eminent in governing; it was he who framed the Codes still in force, and divers laws which have made Costa Rica truly independent. Dr. Don José Maria Castro, patriot, orator, diplomate, and statesman, to whom the country owes largely its advance in political and educational institutions. Don Joaquin Bernardo Calvo,* disinterested and notable statesman; founder of a National journal, who lent his services to the Government, for a period of thirty years, as Minister, Representative, and Senator on various occasions.

Don Vicente Herrera, illustrious as writer and public man.

Don Manuel José Carazo, who contributed largely with his talents to the political march of the country, and to whom is due the organization of the National Hacienda.

Don Francisco Maria Iglesias, patriot and author. In the high posts which he has occupied under the Administration, as delegate, diplomate, or Minister of State, he has labored earnestly and disinterestedly for the good of Costa Rica.

The Licenciate Don Julian Volio, noted for his services to the country, to which he has done honor, whether as diplomate or statesman, in the Government or out of it. One of the most notable orators of the day.

Dr. Don Salvador Jimenez, who stands

---
* Father of the author of this work.

first among political writers of his time; author of the first work on civil rights written in the country.

Don Manuel Maria Peralta, illustrious in diplomatic service and historical productions, possesses in extraordinary degree the gift of memory and the merit of industry, which, combined with clearness of intellect, have given him a fund of political and literary knowledge, by reason of which he is considered in Europe one of the most distinguished of Spanish Americans.

Licenciate Don Leon Fernandez, distinguished as jurisconsulate and author. One of the most striking figures in the politics of the country; indefatigable historian, brilliant diplomate. A great patriot, and in the political struggles courageous and persevering.

Dr. Don Rafael Orozco, jurisconsulate and author, to whose labors are due the present Penal Code. In politics he has held his place in the liberal ranks with laudable persistence. In judicial administration he has filled the high post of President of the Supreme Tribunal.

Licentiate Don Ascension Esquivel; in letters and the National forum he has ably merited the respect and high esteem which he enjoys. As a member of the "Comision Codificadora," his legislative labor shines in the famous Civil Code lately come into force. Of energetic and prudent disposition, his participation in actual politics and diplomacy has merited great praise. Mr. Esquivel is, besides, a forensic orator of easy and elegant delivery.

Licentiate Don Mauro Fernandez; distinguished for his vast knowledge of political and social science, as legislator and Minister of Public Works, and as a political and forensic orator. He is versed in finance, and enthusiastic upon popular education. The advancement of the country in the matter of educational institutions is mainly due to his untiring efforts.

Licentiate Don José J. Rodriguez; talented jurisconsulate; noted for probity of character and prudent and just rulings. A forensic orator of great merit, and a brilliant legislator.

Licentiate Don Ricardo Jimenez; a gentleman of brilliant intellect and extensive information; a strong writer, and ranking with the most distinguished jurisconsulates. He has not thus far occupied himself in politics; but, even at an early age, has most creditably represented Costa Rica and other countries of Central America abroad. He has also occupied the trying position of Secretary of State. In September, 1888, he was appointed to represent Costa Rica in the Central American Congress, which had its sessions at San José; he was elected President of this Congress.

Licentiate Don Cleto Gonzalez Viquez, like Mr. Jimenez, possesses uncommon intellectual powers. As a writer, he ranks among the best of

Costa Rica. He has acted in the capacities of Sub-Secretary of Foreign Affairs, of Secretary of various Legations, and of Chargé d'Affaires for Costa Rica in Washington.

Licentiate Don Pedro Perez Zeledon; author, jurisconsulate, and professor; one of the most brilliant young men in Costa Rica. Intelligent and patriotic, he has filled many responsible posts; has been Sub-Secretary of Hacienda and of Public Instruction; also in the War Department.

Licentiate Don Angel A. Castro; conscientious and correct as writer; eloquent orator; has been Sub-Secretary of *Gobernacion*, and is widely known as jurisconsulate.

Licentiate Don Mauro Aguilar y Coeto, author; Licentiate Don Esequiel Gutierrez, jurisconsulate and diplomate; Don Pio Viquez, author, poet, and orator; Don Faustino Viquez, author of both graceful and solid literature; Licentiate Don Maximo Fernandez, distinguished author, jurisconsulate, and orator; Licentiate Don Manuel Felipe Queros, jurisconsulate and author; Licentiate Don Juan Diego Braun, melodious poet and intelligent lawyer, and Licentiate Don Rafael Montufar, are others of National fame.

Costa Rica may also record with pride the efforts in her behalf made by such eminent Central Americans as: Doctors Don Felipe Molina, Don Nazaris Toledo, Don Lorenzo Montufar, Don Rafael Machado, and Don

Views in San José.
1. The Bishop's Palace.
2. In the Cemetery.
3. Hotel Vigne.

Antonio Cruz; and Don Adolfo Marie, Don Emilio Segura; Dr. Don Miguel Macaya, Dr. Don Fernando Etresber, Dr. Don Valeriano F. Ferraz, Dr. Don Antonio Zambrana, and Dr. Juan F. Ferraz, sons of other nations.

PRINCIPAL TOWNS.

THE CITY OF SAN JOSÉ—CAPITAL OF THE REPUBLIC.

Between the hills of Candelaria and the Barba Mountains, southeast of Irazu, extends the great valley called Abra in the time of the Conquest, and later designated by the names of Valle de Aserri and Valle de Curridabat. In the year 1738, the settlements of Barba and Aserri, situated respectively in the extreme north and south of this valley, formed a single parish. The stony, mountainous road rendered travel difficult, if not dangerous, between the two, and the curé ministering to them sent a communication to the Governor of the Province, showing that in the neighborhood of "Boca del Monte" there were *chacarillas* of sugar-cane and a few scattered houses, and that it would be well to unite the two settlements at that point and form a village.

The suggestion was approved, and some time after the Teniente of Aserri published a proclamation to the effect that all the scattered families unite at *Boca del Monte;* and providing severe penalties for such as failed to comply within a given time. Twenty-one persons were notified, and the town began to be formed with this number.

In 1751 there appeared a cluster of eleven tile-roofed and fifteen thatched houses on a pleasant plain, but having neither streets nor plaza, and with one very poor church. This settlement was called **La Villita**, and its church that of San José, according to Bishop Morel. This gentleman further says that in all the valley there were perhaps 220 tile-roofed and 194 thatched houses; that there were sugar-cane plantations, and that live-stock was raised, and wheat, corn, tobacco, beans, onions, peppers, anise, coriander, and dill were cultivated, and that there were also *chacaras* without care or tillage because of their owners' poverty.

The population was 399 families, with a total of 2,330 persons, "not counting Indians, there being none." The civil government was intrusted to a Teniente (Lieutenant-Governor), and for the military, there were companies of 157 foot soldiers, and one cavalry company numbering 62, with their officers.

These are the earliest data to be had as to the founding of San José.

The establishment in the valley of the tobacco factory gave the province an impulse previously unequaled, developing agriculture, and promoting an advancement desired but unknown in the country.

The town of San José, which, owing to its fertile lands, had grown wonderfully, attracted many residents of Cartago and other places to cultivate tobacco, and so by and by it became of almost equal importance to that of the capital (Cartago); it was thus when, October 16, 1813, the Court of Spain granted it the title of city, as reward of the fidelity shown by it during the insurrection of Salvador and of Granada.

The spirit of progress and desire to excel are observed in San José from its earliest infancy. In the *Tertulia* of October 3, 1834, we read as follows:

"The people of this City of San José being persuaded that knowledge produces all good, and dispels all evil; that from it come good laws, good customs, good government, and that, in short, it is the soul of all happiness, . . . adopted the surest means of combating ignorance in the instruction of youth.

"When the city was no more than a valley, lacking even a municipal council, and, in order to have an authority, it was necessary that Tenientes should come from Cartago, the poor and humble inhabitants had teachers come at considerable cost from the latter city to instruct their young children in the elementary branches. In 1814 teachers were brought from Nicaragua to establish a course of philosophy; in 1815 the Santo Tomas School was established, and shortly after the great *Potrero* of *Las Pavas* was designated for the endowment of elementary education, and a fund begun for Santo Tomas Institute. But all this, instead of meeting with approval and protection from the Government, had to grapple with difficulties consequent on a combat with those in authority."

At the time of Independence, the *Josefinos* (San Joséites) exerted the greatest influence in favor of republican ideas, and, supported by Alajuela and that part of Cartago without nobility interests, dominated completely the situation, and in the year 1823 removed the capital to San José. This measure realized aspirations cherished for some years, and was justified by the central situation of San José, in the most thickly settled part of the country.

The importance of the city made itself ere long apparent; and, without looking with absurd jealousies upon the growth of the other towns, in whose welfare and progress it is interested, it maintains ever its elevated sentiments of fraternity and union.

The present population of the city is 25,000; of the province, 63,406.

The city lies at 9° 56' North Latitude and 84° Longitude west from Greenwich, at an altitude of 3,868 feet above sea-level, bounded on the north by the River Torres, and having the

River Maria Aguilar at a short distance southward. It covers an extent of two kilometers* or more from east to west, and a little less from north to south.

The houses in the principal streets are of one and two stories, present a pleasing appearance, and have modern conveniences. Recently brick has been adopted for building purposes in place of the old-style adobe or *bajareque.*

The streets, formed without determined plan, present some irregularities, but not of a nature to affect their good order. They were first paved with stone in 1837, through the zeal of Don José Rafael Gallegos, special commissioner of the municipality; but this system leaving much to be desired, from the nature of the land, the substitution of macadam has been going on, until to-day it is found throughout almost all the city. The streets are some ten meters wide, and in some of them there are unevenness or slight rises caused by conditions of the earth.

The principal streets are: Comercio, Cuño, Carrillo, Calvo, and Fabrica, on the north; University, Seminary, and Velarde, or Cemetery Street, on the south; Cathedral, General Fernandez Street, Merced, Teatro, and Uruca, on the west; and Laberinto, Goicoechea, and Vapor, on the east.

Drinking water (and water for general use)

---
*1 kilometer = ⅔ of a mile.

comes to San José from a considerable distance; is deposited in and filtered through five handsome reservoirs, thence distributed by iron pipes, permitting all conveniences. The system was constructed under the supervision of Engineer Don Angel Miguel Velasquez, in 1867, during the second administration of Don José Maria Castro. In the public plazas there are fountains, as also in the court-yards of many public edifices and private houses.

Various difficulties have prevented the construction of sewers, for which reason this improvement is yet lacking; they are undertaking to establish a system of portable apparatus for the collection and removal of refuse matter, by contract.

Street lighting was established in San José in 1840. It consisted then of lanterns provided with tallow candles, whose feeble light lasted but a few hours. This poor method was replaced by that of oil in 1856, and according as the city progressed, good lamps were arranged to the number of 225 in the central part. These, again, were superseded by electric light, adopted by special contract, whose service is universal throughout the city, and whose light is a hundred times superior. It is hoped that ere long incandescent lighting may be adopted for the houses.

The police, with a view to better discipline, is organized militarily. It is composed of a first commandante, a second commandante, six sergeants, and eighty *gens d'armes*, provided with all that good service demands, including a proper uniform. This department, which was formerly almost useless through neglect and poor organization, is to-day regulated in accordance with the legislation of model countries, and affords important services.

The principal public buildings of the capital are:

The National Palace.
The Presidential Palace.
The new Palace of Justice.
The Bishop's Palace.
The University.
The Seminary-College.
The College of Sion.
The Orphan Asylum.
The Principal Cuartel.
The National Liquor Factory.

Of churches, the Cathedral alone may be cited for beauty and elegance of architecture. The Church of La Carmen comes next, for solidity of construction in iron and masonry. The Church of Mercedes is another, and those of Soledad and Dolores are being built.

The Protestant place of worship is a beautiful little gothic chapel. [Set in a garden overflowing with trees and rose-bushes constantly in bloom, with eternal azure above, and the breeze of eternal summer blowing softly through the open windows, it were hard to find a lovelier or more peaceful spot to enter on the Sabbath.—Ed.]

A short distance from the Cathedral is the Masonic Temple, erected in 1868.

The market of San José is well built and capacious. The need of another such is felt at the other end of the town. The slaughter-house provides desirable meats, the sole fault noted being a lack of suitable vehicles for the conveyance of meat to places where it is sold.

The railway station, with its fine work-shops, is to be, also, the street railway station. The buildings are plain, but admirably adapted for their purpose.

The public offices are all more or less well lodged. The want is felt, however, of buildings especially arranged for the National Archives, the Central Customs, the Inspection General of Hacienda, the Artillery Cuartel, the Department of Statistics, the Mint, and the National Printing House.

The principal charitable institutions of San José are under the management of corporations or unions constantly laboring to improve them.

The Hospital of San Juan de Dios does credit to Costa Rica. It was founded in 1799, by Bishop Tristan, and met vicissitudes which made its maintenance uncertain until 1852; in that year it was firmly established, and it has since become an institution from whose doors no one in need of shelter and succor is turned away. Not far from this is the Hospital for Women.

The Lepers' Hospital accommodates all the unfortunates of the country who, because of their affliction, can not live with the rest of humanity. The building was donated by the Government.

The Orphan Asylum for Girls was established in 1869, by Doña Maria Montealegre, according to the will of Doña Jeronima Fernandez de Montealegre; it receives destitute female children, and in its shelter educates them and prepares them for occupations in keeping with their circumstances.

The Hospital for Incurables, founded in 1879, is especially designed for the aged poor.

A fine building is being erected for an Idiot Asylum. The Charitable Association, with the Government's support, has effected this measure by means of a lottery. Great credit is due the members of this organization—particularly Don Carlos Duran and Licenciado Don Gerardo Castro—for energy and disinterested labors. The institution will not only be one whose necessity has long been felt, but the building will prove an ornament to the city. It will occupy the center of handsome grounds.

The cemeteries are under the supervision of the Charitable Association. They are beautifully kept, and contain many fine tombs and vaults.

Commercially, San José very naturally maintains supremacy. It is the residence of the wealthiest merchants, and in it are the three banks, Anglo-Costarricense, Union, and Costa Rica; also the office of the Mining Company of Monte del Aguacate, that of the Agency Companies, that of the Market Company, and that of the Bella Vista Baths Company.

It contains eight first-class warehouses, seventeen principal stores, thirty-two smaller, and fifty second-class; there are three breweries, seven wood factories, also tobacco and aguardiente and other little shops; there are a hundred grocery and liquor stores; there are four good libraries and stationery stores, and, for convenience in business, there are eleven offices of brokers and commission dealers. There are also jeweler stores, tailor-shops, shoe-shops and barber-shops, in European style. There are several factories, the National Liquor Factory being unrivaled throughout Central America.

The University contains the only National Library; there are 3,000 volumes, scientific and miscellaneous works. Don Miguel Obregon L., with the assistance of the Department of Instruction, has labored hard to increase the number of books, and deserves great credit for his zeal.

The theatre does not correspond with the city's advance otherwise. About its only merit is that of being the first built in Central America. A new one is hoped for.

The public promenades most frequented are the Central Park and the Parque de la Estacion. The erection is contemplated of a hippodrome, with various amusements, in the savanna of Mata Redonda,* near the city. In connection with this, the street railway will be laid connecting the hippodrome with the city center, the market, the Custom House, and the railway station.

The International Club membership includes the greater part of the Costaricans. It occupies spacious quarters, has fine reception and reading-rooms, with newspapers in various languages, and a library of 5,000 volumes. The Commercial Club stands next in importance. It has 200 members.

The San José Philharmonic is a musical society, with many members, including several professors and a number of young ladies and gentlemen. It has contributed largely to the advancement and cultivation of the taste for music, particularly as to the piano and singing.

There are scientific societies of law and medicine, also a scientific literary association, "El Porrenir."

The principal hotels are:

Gran Hotel, Don C. de Benedictis, proprietor.

---
*A splendid stretch of open meadow, with indescribably lovely mountain views in every direction.—ED.

Hotel Frances, Don José Vigne, proprietor.
Hotel Victor, Don Victor Aubert, proprietor.
Hotel de Roma, Don José Sacripanti, proprietor.

Café and Restaurant de Paris, Rava and Allard, proprietors.

They have modern conveniences, airy parlors, and provide excellent tables.

San José is also the capital of the province of that name, and the head town of the canton. The province, as already shown, is divided in six cantons. For agricultural importance, after San José, that of Desamparados comes first, and Escasu second. The two villages of the same names as these cantons have fine streets, handsome churches, and good houses as a rule.

Pacaca and Aserri, head villages of the cantons of same names, have existed since the time of the discovery of the country.

The Canton of Puriscal is destined to have a great future, by reason of the wonderful fertility of its lands and its nearness to the coast.

CARTAGO.

The City of Cartago, situated in the beautiful valley of that name (the old Valley of Guarco), at the foot of the Volcano Irazu, and at 4,930 feet above sea-level, is one of the best-located towns in Costa Rica. Its climate is cool and pleasant, its healthfulness unremitting, its soil fertile, its streams pure and beautiful;

Church of the Angels, at Cartago.

these and the delightful aspect of scenery and surroundings render Cartago a place where the spirit is revived and the body newly strengthened.

Cartago was founded in 1563, by the conqueror of Costa Rica, Don Juan Vasquez de Coronado, who, in 1565, speaking of the locality, said that the natives were spirited, war-like, large in stature, and well-formed, similar to the Mexicans in their movements, and possessed good cotton clothing and gold of all grades in great quantities. The tombs unearthed in the vicinity would indicate that the Indians were indeed rich in gold, and that they possessed remarkable artistic abilities. Don J. R. R. Troya, of Cartago, owns a fine collection of these antiquities.

In 1636 the city had progressed considerably, and contained some wealthy citizens, who trafficked direct with the Peninsula. The town was divided in two parts. The Spaniards occupied one and the *mulatos* the other, a boundary mark being fixed for the latter, known as the *Cruz de caravaca*, which still exists.

Of the apparition of the Virgin of the Angels, which occurred August 2, 1643, a pious tradition relates that in the district inhabited by the dusky-skinned, upon a rock, from beneath which a spring gushed forth, a *mulata* woman, going to fetch wood, found a little image, which she took home with her and guarded safely in her house. Returning to the spring next day, she found another such image, which she took home to compare with the first. To her surprise, the first found had vanished. The third day the second image had disappeared mysteriously. A priest was made acquainted with the facts, and repaired, with various citizens, to the fountain, where a third time the image was discovered. It was declared to be a miraculous manifestation of the Virgin of the Angels, and construed as a sign that a church be erected upon the spot, which was afterward done.

The decadence of Costa Rica and the eruption of Irazu in 1723, considerably lessened the importance and population of the city.

In 1738 its best neighborhood was reduced to four or five families. There was not then a single school; but there was the Parochial Church, with two curés, the Convent of San Francisco, with sixteen religious brothers, and four little churches, those of San Nicolas, San Juan, La Soledad, and Los Angeles, assisted by fourteen other clergymen.

This year, although the water ran by and into the houses, the streets were not paved, but the bad places only mended, so that processions might pass.

There was no meat sold publicly, nor was there any circulation of money. They dealt with cocoa or made exchanges.

In 1751 the part occupied by the Spaniards counted but ninety-seven tile-roof houses and forty-seven thatched, and the cleanliness and care of the churches was neglected. The other part of town contained 103 thatched houses, arranged in streets, and the temple consecrated to the Virgin, which was carefully tended.

At the west of the city was a small district called Laborio, with twenty-six houses in four streets, to-day forming part of the city.

The population of Cartago was then 626 families, with 4,289 persons.

In 1751 the militia of Cartago included a field master, sergeant-major, a general aid, and "three of the third;" four companies of foot soldiers (one, *Guzmanes*, two of *mestizos*, and one of *pardos*, or dark-colored men) and one of cavalry, with their officers; it consisted of 474 soldiers.

The earthquake of 1841 destroyed the city completely; it was rebuilt the following year, according to the plan made by Don Simon Orozco and approved by President Don Braulio Carrillo. It stands thus at present.

The principal buildings are:

The Principal Cuartel, built in 1865.

The Municipal Palace and the College of San Luis, which are among the best municipal buildings in the Republic; also the College del Carazon de Jesus.

The city has six elegant churches, built of

stone at great cost; those of Los Angeles, of San Francisco, of Carmen, and of San Nicolas, notable for their gothic architecture; those of Soledad and Guadalupe; and there is in course of erection a grand parochial church, to cost $60,000.

The water-works system is modern; the houses are supplied with iron pipes, and there are fountains in the squares. The streets are wide, straight, and excellently paved.

The city is very quiet, owing to the retired character of its inhabitants. It was the capital of Costa Rica until 1823.

The College of San Luis was in 1869 an honor to Central America. The Licenciado Jimenez, as Governor of Cartago, laid the first stone of the edifice, and it fell to his lot, as President of the Republic, to inaugurate it.

There is a school, founded by the Rev. Don José F. Peralto, and sustained with funds supplied by this distinguished gentleman.

There are, at present, in the principal canton, thirty-one primary schools, for both sexes, sustained by the Government. There are also private schools, among them one for young ladies. Higher education is received at the San Louis College, which is sustained municipally.

Cartago has a musical society, the "Euterpe."

There are no charitable institutions except the hospital, founded by certain philanthropists. There are a great many mendicants.

The city is perhaps at present a little more disposed to animation than formerly. This in consequence of the work going on upon the new railway branch thence to Limon.

Various enterprises have been undertaken, among which are the "Baths of Bella Vista," shortly to be opened to the public.

Cartago is the capital of the province of that name, and head city of the principal canton of the same. The province includes, also, the Canton of Paraiso (chief village, Paraiso) and Canton of Tres Rios (chief village, La Union). The Village of Paraiso was founded in 1832, by the inhabitants of the Valley of Ujarraz, in consequence of an epidemic raging in that valley.

La Union Village, in 1751, was composed of seven thatched houses, in which there dwelt forty Indians brought from Talamanca. To-day it is one of the most important villages in the country, having most valuable coffee lands.

Its situation, cool climate, good streams, straight streets, and handsome parochial church attract attention.

The present population of the city is 12,000 (approximately); of the province, 33,889.

ALAJUELA.

The City of Alajuela, like that of Heredia, is situated among the foot-hills of Barba, and toward the extreme northwest of the line formed by the principal towns of the Republic.

This first became a city in November, 1824. It is situated in a beautiful plain. It has fifteen streets from east to west and eleven from north to south. Of the first, Guardia, Soto, Padre Corral, Alfaro Ruiz, and Juan Santamaria Streets are the best; and of the second, Estacion, General Fernandez, and Alfaro Streets.

The parochial church has few rivals in the country, as to construction. The cuartel, built under the administration of Gen. Don Tomas Guardia, is the best of its kind in Costa Rica. The Municipal Palace is an imposing edifice. The Alajuela Institute and the National College are also of importance. The plazas and parks have fine fountains, and the general supply of water is good.

The Province of Alajuela is divided in six cantons. Alajuela is the principal canton, and Alajuela City the chief town. Grecia, head village of Grecia Canton, is a great agricultural center. In the Village of San Ramon there is a library, and various papers have been published. There is a handsome palace in course of erection for the public offices. It will doubtless be the next village to receive the title of city. The Village of Naranjo possesses rich lands and wide-awake inhabitants.

The present population of the Alajuela city is 9,000; of the province, 51,087.

HEREDIA.

The City of Heredia is in the foot-hills of the Barba Mountains, northwest from San José, and between the Rivers Pirro and Quebrada del Burio. In 1751 it contained twenty-four houses, a cabilda, and a church, all adobe and tile-roofed, and sixty-nine thatched houses, in four streets running east and west and five north and south. Its territorial boundaries comprised five leagues of width and three of breadth, containing fifty-seven tile-roofed houses and 337 thatched, and having farms, husbandry, and fruit equal to those of San José. There were 496 families, with 3,116 persons, no Indians included.

The first canton has eighteen elementary schools, with over 3,000 pupils of both sexes, and for higher education there are the College of San Augustin and the Heredia College. The perimeter of the city includes four squares of a manzana each, divided by four streets from north to south and four from east to west, the most important of which is the one leading to the railway depot. The two churches are imposing.

The water-works system is the first of the kind introduced into the country. A market building is contemplated, to be connected by street railway with the railway station.

Heredia has a literary and scientific association, "El Estudio," which has achieved considerable reputation in the country.

The present population of the city is 9,000; of the Province of Heredia, 29,409.

Heredia City, head city of the principal canton, is the capital of the province of the same name, which contains, also, the Cantons of Barba, Santo Domingo, Santa Barbara, and San Rafael. The Village of Barba is one of the oldest in Costa Rica. Its proximity to the rise of the River Sarapaqui augurs well for its future. The Village of Santo Domingo contains the bluest-blooded families and most beautiful women of Costa Rica. Santa Barbara, between Barba and Alajuela, is another village looking forward to a great future, when it shall communicate easily by the San Carlos and Sarapaqui with the San Juan and the north. The Canton of San Rafael is also productive in a high degree.

LIBERIA, SANTA CRUZ, AND NICOYA.

The extensive Province of Guanacaste, ancient division of Nicoya, comprises an important section of the Republic, from the variety of its products and its topographical position. The province includes five cantons: Liberia, Nicoya, Santa Cruz, Bagaces, and Las Canas. Santa Cruz is first in order of population, Liberia and Nicoya next.

The City of Liberia is the capital of the province; its central location and advancement have made it so. Its population is 5,692. Santa Cruz and Nicoya are in the great cape (or peninsula) which protects the Gulf of Nicoya, and have 5,697 and 4,588 inhabitants, respectively.

Stock-farming and the felling of timber are the principal occupations of the inhabitants.

The Government is at present considering the question of more rapid and easy communication than now exists between these regions and the interior.

PART II.

DISCOVERY AND CONQUEST OF COSTA RICA.

SPANISH RULE UNTIL 1821, AND PRINCIPAL EVENTS DOWN TO THE ORGANIZATION OF THE FIRST REGULAR GOVERNMENT, IN 1825.

FIRST PERIOD.

SPANISH RULE.—DISCOVERY AND CONQUEST OF COSTA RICA, 1502 TO 1565.

On the 9th of May, 1502, the immortal Columbus left Cadiz upon his fourth and last voyage to the world he had discovered. Five small vessels, with a crew of 150, formed the squadron which conducted to the Central American shores the first Spaniards who set foot upon the soil. When near the Island of Santo Domingo, a tempest put them in imminent peril, and separated the five ships; but these coming together again at the west of the island, and having repaired their damages, they arrived on July 30th at La Guanaja, the first spot of Central America touched by Columbus, to which he himself gave the name "Isla de los Pinos," and which to-day belongs to Honduras. Sunday, August 14th, he landed with some of his companions in Caxinas (to-day Trujillo), and that day mass was celebrated for the first time in that country. The 17th of the same August, Columbus, having entered the River Tinto in small boats, unfurled the royal flag of Spain, and took possession of the land in the name of the King of Castile. Thus were consummated the two acts which inaugurated the religious and the political transformation of these lands.

They were continuing their journey southward, when a furious tempest arose, in which they nearly perished. Columbus, in describing it to the King of Spain, said: "There have been other storms, but none of such duration or violence." The 12th of September they doubled the Cape of Gracias a Dios, which the Admiral so named because of the calming of the tempest there; the ships were repaired, and, continuing their voyage, they arrived at last— October 5, 1502—at the region which to-day is the Republic of Costa Rica. It was the first spot in Central America where the Spaniards found the object of their solicitude—gold. The natives used it in different forms as ornaments. The illustrious Genoese discovered all the Atlantic coast of Costa Rica, the Islands and Bay of Almirante, thus named in his honor; traversed the *terra firma* surrounding these islands, which he called *Vera Aqua*, and returned to Spain, after having searched as far as Portobelo for the channel which he believed to exist between the two oceans.

As will be seen, the various tribes of Indians who inhabited the country at the time of its discovery, if they had not attained the same progress as others of America, still had advanced to a certain grade of civilization, attested by the fortifications which the Spaniards found in the Village of Couto, and by the fact of their using gold as a medium of exchange.

The population was estimated at 40,000 to 60,000 inhabitants, distributed in different settlements in Nicoya and Los Chomes; in Garabito, Catapas, Tices y Los Botos, comprising the region south of Lake Nicaragua and San Juan River to the confluence of Sarapaqui, and east from the Gulf of Nicoya as far as the Barba Mountains; in the Valley of Coyoche, between the Rivers Barranca and Rio Grande, as far as the Volcano Herradura; over the Abra o Curiraba y Toyopan, which is the valley in which are found San José and Curridabat; in the Guarco, which is the Valley of Cartago; in Tiro and Corroci (Atirro and Orosi); in Accerri y Pacaqua in Quepos, at the south of Candelaria, four leagues from the Pacific; in Turucaca Couto or Coto, and others of the great valley where are found Terraba and Boruca; in Talamanca and its vicinity; in the Valley of Guaymi, opposite the Escudo de Veragua, and as far as Chiriqui River; in Pococi, which comprises the Valley of Matina, or Chirripo, and the Punta Blanca, north of where the town of

Limon is, and in Suerre, which lies between the Sarapaqui, San Juan, and Reventazon Rivers.

Diego de Nicuesa was the first Spaniard who engaged in the colonization of the territory which is now Costa Rica. That distinguished gentleman, fascinated by the stories of great riches in Veragua, and being appointed Governor of the same place in 1509, repaired to that region. He visited the Bay of Almirante, and named the island, which ever since has been known as "Escudo de Veragua," upon which, abandoned to misery and despair, he was at the point of perishing, and not long after, as related by some of his companions, he succumbed, victim to a series of misfortunes and hostilities of his own compatriots.

The Southern Ocean was discovered September 26, 1513, by Vasco Nuñez de Balboa. Then came Pedrarias de Avila, appointed Governor of Castilla del Oro, and devoted his whole attention to exploring the Pacific coast. He sent out Captains Gaspar de Espinosa (who discovered Burica and the Gulf of Osa, now Golfo Dulce), Juan de Castaneda, Hernan Ponce de Leon, and Bartolome de Hurtado, who skirted the coast as far as the Gulf of Nicoya in 1519, in two ships constructed on the Island of Perlas, Bay of Panama, by Vasco Nuñez de Balboa, the first to sail the Ocean of the South.

Later, in 1522, Gil Gonzalez de Avila traversed on foot all the territory of Costa Rica from Chiriqui; he discovered Nicaragua, which was conquered by Francisco Hernandez de Cordova; at the same time that Pedro de Alvarada established the dominion of Spain in Guatemala, Cristobal de Olid penetrated into Honduras, and Diego de Mazariegos entered Chiapas, as Teniente of Hernan Cortez, in 1523 and 1524.

In January, 1523, Francisco Hernandez founded the City of Bruselas,* near the Gulf of Nicoya, this being the first colony established in Costa Rica. A little later, in 1526, Pedrarias de Avila in person took possession of the Isle of Chira, in Nicoya Gulf, thus beginning the conquest of all the territory which later constituted the Kingdom of Guatemala.

Hernan Sanchez de Badajoz, appointed Governor of Costa Rica in 1539, arrived with his suite at the mouth of the River Teliri (Sicsola) at the end of April, 1540, and without delay founded the City of Badajoz, on the banks of the same river, and two months later a fortification in Corotapa, also called Marbella. Badajoz was closing the conquest of Talamanca, when, in November of the same year, the Governor of Nicaragua, Rodrigo de Contreras, with 100 Spaniards and 200 Indians which he brought from Nicaragua, claimed the territory as his domain, obliged him (Badajoz) to suspend his conquest, accused him, and sent

---

* Destroyed by order of Diego Lopez de Salcedo, 1527.

him to the Council of Indians for judicial sentence, March 5, 1541.

Diego Gutierrez, appointed Governor of Cartago, lost two years in disputes with Rodrigo de Contreras; but, being reconciled with the latter through the intervention of the Bishop of Nicaragua, in November, 1543, entered by the River Suerre, and made a show of founding the City of Talamanca. Lack of resources obliged him to return to Desaguadero (River San Juan); there he received some provisions from Captain Barrientos, and sent, in the latter's boat, his nephew, Alonso de Pisa, to bring people from Nombre de Dios.

After many difficulties, occasioned by bad weather, at the close of September, 1544, Gutierrez and his men, by means of a frigate and four boats, ascended thirty miles up the same river, where he found some houses, and lodged himself in one of them, belonging to the principal inhabitant of Suerre.

He named these cottages the City of San Francisco, having arrived at the site the 4th of October. His behavior there, and the infamies he committed, obliged him to proceed inland, ascending partly by the same river as far as Tayutic, five leagues from Cartago, where, in the rising of the Indians of that place, he was killed in battle, which obliged the Spaniards to retire again to San Juan.

There afterward came Licenciado Juan de

Cavallon, and the clergyman Juan de Estrada Ravago, who organized their expedition to Nicaragua in the year 1560, Ravago supplying the necessary funds, as Cavallon had none.

The Padre Estrada Ravago departed with four ships for the San Juan, and directed his course toward the Bay of San Jeronimo (Zarabaro, to-day Bay Almirante), where the same year he founded, with sixty Spaniards, the "Villa del Castillo de Austria;" afterward he passed the Port of Suerre, and thence took his course to Nicaragua, whence he came to Nicoya to meet Cavallon again. The latter had come by land to explore the sea-coast of the South, and founded, January, 1561, in the district of Chorotega, or Valle del Coyoche, the Village of Landecho, in honor of Don Juan Martinez de Landecho, President of the *Audiencia* of Guatemala. The Village of Landecho, also called Villa de los Reyes, was situated four leagues from the coast and its port, Landecho (to-day known as Caldera).

Three days' journey from this village toward the interior, he founded, in March of the same year, another settlement, to which he gave the name City of the Castillo de Garci-Muñoz. There were no Indians in the vicinity; the soil was miry, and the highlands rocky and sterile; notwithstanding these difficulties, the City of Castillo de Garci-Muñoz was of great assistance in the conquest of the rest of the country.

Juan Vasquez de Coronado, native of Salamanca, born in 1525, was without doubt the real conqueror of Costa Rica. Belonging to an illustrious family, and educated carefully in the best days of the famous university of his country, Vasquez de Coronado is distinguished among those made celebrated by their exploits in the New World. He did not come to Central America as an adventurer, but when he arrived at Guatemala, in 1550, he was provided with a royal warrant as Licenciado Cerrato, in which it is ordered the President of the Audience of Boundaries shall occupy himself in public duties of honor and profit, and is highly recommended. He held, among other positions, that of first Alcalde of Salvador and Honduras, and later of Nicaragua, that of Alcalde Ordinary of Guatemala City, and in April, 1562, he was appointed Alcalde Mayor of the Provinces of Cartago and Costa Rica. When he arrived in this Province he found the Spaniards in great need, and divided among them material for clothing, arms, saddle equipments, and other necessaries, and immediately sent his captains to treat peaceably with the head inhabitants of Garabito y Coyoche.

His expedition to Talamanca was undoubtedly the most notable of all; he carried it out from the Port of Coronado all the way across the country, "crossing the highest part of the cordillera that separates the two oceans, from the summit of which both were plainly seen."

In Talamanca he was received peaceably, as he usually was, by the Indians. Among the chiefs who presented themselves and offered allegiance to the new master was Siestoli, a Mexican established there with some of his compatriots. Without evincing an undue greed for gold, which metal they knew to be abundant in the *comarca*, the beds of the rivers and ravines of the Duy Valley were examined, and from the principal stream there were obtained specimens of the finest quality in sufficient quantity to assure the wealth of the locality. Coronado then named this river Rio de la Estrella.

Talamanca being explored, they took possession in 1564 of the Bay del Almirante, of the Valley of Guaymi, of the Rio de la Estrella, and of all the tribes included in that vast territory.

The founding of Cartago City is one of the most notable events of that period, and of those which made Coronado famous. His important services attracted the attention of the King, and in 1565 Vasquez de Coronado, being then in Spain, was appointed Governor and Captain-general of Costa Rica, and facilities accorded him for carrying out his undertaking. He was also appointed Governor of Nicaragua for three years, in order to assist him in the settlement of Costa Rica.

While returning to Costa Rica, accompanied by numerous gentlemen from Salamanca, a storm arose, in which they were all shipwrecked, and lost.

From the expeditions of Vasquez de Coronado, the territory of Costa Rica became known almost in its entirety, and the Indians had acknowledged allegiance to their new masters without great battles and bloodshed. There were many clergymen who lent valuable assistance toward the peaceful conquest, and who labored earnestly to convert the Indians. Among these were Pedro Alonso and Juan de Betanzos, Juan Pizarro, Lorenzo de Bienvenida, Martin de Bonilla, and others.

Fray Pedro Alonso de Betanzos came to America in 1542, among the 200 friars composing a mission to Guatemala. He was the founder of the Convent of San Francisco at Cartago. He died in Chomes, in 1570, and his remains were taken to Cartago, and interred in the convent he had founded. In the earthquake of 1841 his ashes were lost.

The Padre Juan Pizarro died in 1586, a victim to the fury of the natives. He was preaching on the day of the Immaculate Conception in an Indian village, when a party of Indians attacked him, stripped him, beat him unmercifully, and tortured him until he died. His body was hurled over a precipice by his torturers.

In 1568, Perafau de Rivera, who became Governor of Costa Rica, founded the port of his name on the west coast of the Gulf of Nicoya, and the City of Aranjuez, which he located not far from where had been that of Bruselas; he also founded the city of the name of Jesus, in the vicinity of the Isle of Caño, after his exploration of the Atlantic coast, and made the division of patronage between the conquerors, disposing of the following villages:

Garabito, of the Coyoche Valley; of those of Real, Pereyra, Barba, Yuruste, Coboboci, Abacara, and Chucasque, on the Rio Grande, all of which formed the Province of Garabito, with 2,500 population of Indians. The Province of Curiraba, with 600 Indians; Quirco, with 150; Coo, with 350; Uxarraci, including Turichiqui, 300; Turrialba and Little Turrialba, with more than 2,000 Indians; Pacaca, with 1,600; Quepo, with 1,000; Cocto, with 800; Boruca, with 250; Cabra, with 250; Tabiquiri, with 150; Accerri, with over 1,000; Oroci, with over 150; Buxebux, with over 200; Purapura, with over 50; Corroci, with over 200; Atirro and Tayutic, largely populated, and also the villages of Pariagua, Carucap, Duxua, Caraquibou, Pococi, Aoyaque, Guacara, Ibacara, Chirripo, Uxua, Auaca, Bexu, Curbubite, Abacitaba, Arira, Xupragua, Moyagua, Tariaca, Aracara, Mesabaru, and Bore.

Rivera was succeeded by Antonio Pereira,

and he in turn by Alonso de Anguciana y Gamboa, both these being provisional governors. Gamboa took great interest in the progress of Costa Rica, and after removing the City of Aranjuez to the Coyocho Valley, founded the new Village of Castillo de Austria, in the Port of Suerre. Gamboa was succeeded by Diego de Artieda Cherino. Artieda had instructions to inspect the coast in search of English buccaneers, and, having traversed the Atlantic coast line for this purpose, and not having found any, he landed at the mouth of a river which he named Rio de Nuestra Senora, of the Valley of Guaymi. Ascending it for some two or three leagues, he founded upon its banks colonies, one of which he named City of Artieda of the new Kingdom of Navarra, and upon a tree, in the spot selected for plaza, he put a cross, with "In the name of the Father, of the Son, and of the Holy Ghost" inscribed upon it.

He also founded Esparza in 1578.

The famous pirate, Francis Drake, was on the Pacific coast in 1579; he anchored his ships before the Port of Coronado and the Island of Caño, knowing that he was protected by the Court of England.

Artieda's government might have proved of great benefit to Costa Rica; but he could not realize his projects, nor complete the work begun toward the conquest of Talamanca, since the Audience of Guatemala kept it in constant inquietude until his death, in 1590.

FOUNDING OF THE FAMOUS CITY OF SANTIAGO DE TALAMANCA — ITS DESTRUCTION AND OTHER EVENTS FROM 1605 TO 1665—NEW PROJECTS OF CONQUEST OF TALAMANCA.

Artieda Cherino was succeeded by various provisional governors; then came Fernando de la Cuera, who was succeeded by Gonzalo Vasquez de Coronado, a son of Juan Vasquez de Coronado. This one had inherited the title of "Adelantado" from his father. He began to govern in 1601.

It was proposed to make a road from Cartago to Santiago Alanje, Chiriqui, in order to assure dominion over the villages Boruca and Cocto, or Couto; but they did not succeed in crossing the cordilleras as far as the streams flowing to the Atlantic. This undertaking was carried out by his successor, Don Juan de Ocon y Trillo, in 1605, its execution being intrusted to Diego de Sojo y Peñaranda, who entered Talamanca without bloodshed, and subdued the villages of Ateo, Viceita, Terrebe, Cururu, Quequexque, Usabaru, Sacaque, and others, and on October 10, 1605, at 9 in the morning, he founded the City of Talamanca, near the River Sicsola (Tarire), about eight leagues from the Atlantic, the Rio de la Estrella being on the east of the city.

Gonzalo Vasquez de Coronado had concluded an agreement with the President of the Audience of Guatemala, by which he received the title of Governor of the Duy Valley and of the Mexicans, with private jurisdiction in the City of Santiago, independent of that of the Government of Costa Rica, and with obligation to conclude the conquest of the rest of Talamanca.

His undertaking was highly successful, according to the following data: The vessels entered by the river as far as the Castle of San Ildefonso, where they were loaded, passed out, and in three days' time reached Portobelo. In Talamanca there was a great deal of cocoa, potatoes, honey and wax, sarsaparilla, and hemp from which they made the ropes for the vessels. It is certain that gold was abundant, the greatest quantities being found in Corotopa, in or near the River Estrella. The fine kinds of wood permitted the construction of vessels in the river, and these must have been of regular burden, since they made the voyages above mentioned. The population of Talamanca was estimated at 25,000, including the different tribes.

The year 1610 found Don Gonzalo in the City of Cartago, old and feeble, and Diego de Sojo y Peñaranda as Teniente in Talamanca.

Sojo went out one day, with twenty-five soldiers, to make raids among the Jicagua, Mayagua, and Cabecara tribes, and in consequence of his having beaten and cut off the ears of various chiefs, pretending that they were not going to serve the residents of Santiago, and because of his having attacked and robbed an Indian temple of its golden idols, the Indians, enraged at this great sacrilege, attacked Sojo and his followers, killing some and wounding others. Sojo would have sought refuge in Santiago, but on the way there he learned that the city was besieged by the Indians, and, instead of going to its aid, he went to Tariaca (Chirripo), whence he sent word to the Governor of Cartago.

The Indians destroyed and burned the city, and the Spaniards took refuge in the fort of San Ildefonso, which, though of wood and thatch, protected them against the enemy. These troubles occurred in July, 1610. There were various projects, after this, for undertaking anew the conquest, but none were carried out. In May, 1638, Don Gregorio Sandoral, then Governor, proposed the conquest, but with no result. Instead, he carried out the opening of a road to the Port of Matina, or Punta Blanca, in 1636, a road which naturally affected the prosperity of the Province. With the duties from this port could be paid his salary and the salaries of the priests, without applying to Nicaragua as formerly.

In those days the old River of Suerre was very deep; but in 1630 most of its waters went into the Reventazon, and the Port of Suerre remained useless until, in 1651, the Governor, Don Juan Fernandez de Salinas y Cerda, had the outlets, where the water was diverted, closed, reëstablished the port, and built a custom house, thus expediting communication with Portobelo and Cartagena. In 1652 this Governor asked authority to conquer Talamanca, but it was not granted him. In 1659 he was succeeded by Don Andres Arias Maldonado, Field Master, who undertook to effect some progress in Talamanca; but it was only in 1661 that Rodrigo Arias Maldonado y Velazco undertook anew the conquest, and founded the Village of San Bartolome, near the River Telire.

He might have achieved great success, through his ability to manage the Indians, if he could have obtained the appointment of Governor proper; but this was impossible, and his comrades abandoned him to perish.

The expenses of the expedition were borne by him in person, and by great risk and exertion he was able to found some villages, where he built temples and placed priests to preach the Christian religion.

These valuable services were rewarded with the title of Marquis of Talamanca.

DECAY OF THE PROVINCE—1666 TO 1727.

The Province had arrived at a satisfactory grade of prosperity, and although thus far the

Spanish population was not large, its excellent climate and the richness of its soil should have attracted many colonies. Commerce was flourishing through the Port of Matina, on the Atlantic, with Portobelo, Cartagena, and other places, and through the Port of Caldera, on the Pacific, with Panama, Peru, and other countries.

The exports were cattle, horses, mules, hogs, salt meats, tallow, hemp, and provisions of all kinds. The opening of the road to Matina had given good results. The cultivation of cocoa in that valley had extended vastly.

Unfortunately, from 1665 the depredations of pirates had caused great inquietude among the inhabitants, and the progress, hardly under way, met with great difficulties; it even went so far that the extreme measure of closing the ports to foreign commerce was reached. Little else was done during the government of Juan Lopez de la Flor than to defend the Province.

The attempts of the corsairs did not amount merely to sacking and pillaging, but they had the idea of possessing themselves of the country and establishing communication from sea to sea. In this they were supported by the English Governor of Jamaica. With this motive, the buccaneers **Morgan** and **Mansfelt**, in 1666, prepared a formal expedition; they arrived at Matina with 500 to 800 men, in fifteen ships, landed, and made their way to the interior as far as Turrialba.

Warned in time, the Governor went forth to put them to rout and to close the narrow pass at the opening of Quebrada Honda, where he arrived April 15th. There he strengthened his forces to over 400 men, having received word that the filibusters had arrived at Turrialba.

Mansfelt being apprised of the presence of the forces at Quebrada Honda, commanded by Sergeant-major Don Alonso de Bonilla, of the distance to Cartago, and the kind of roads they would have to travel, decided to retreat; but while they remained there they shot all the cattle and mules they could find in the place, and destroyed everything they could get hold of.

The retreat was rapid, and although Governor Lopez de la Flor pressed forward and sent men to pursue them, they soon had passed the River Suerre and gained the safety of their ships. Bonilla followed them as far as Matina, but only found the prisoners that Mansfelt had set at liberty in his flight.

This was the most formidable attempt made by the corsairs to gain possession of Costa Rica, or to cross it and submit it to pillage.

The constant alarm felt by the inhabitants caused such as did not emigrate to establish themselves in the interior, subject to a miserable commerce with Nicaragua and Panama; their poverty augmented until they were reduced to a lamentable condition. In 1668 the price of meat was a real for thirteen pounds, and this not paid in metals, but in grains of cocoa.

With this condition of affairs began the government of Don Juan Francisco Saenz Vasquez, inaugurated in 1674, who immediately began his efforts to lift Costa Rica out of her troubles.

Saenz was enterprising, and desired the prosperity of the Province. He decided that there should be an end of the constant inquietude of the people, caused by the pirates Sharp, Dampier, and others, and in order to provide the people with means of defense against invasions —there not being fifty arms in good condition in all the country—he procured 200 fire-arms from Panama and various other war appliances.

In June, 1676, the enemy, leaving its armada in Portete (Moin), entered by the Matina River in pirogues, with 800 men, and took possession of the valley. The Governor, being apprised, set forth with 500 soldiers and 200 Indian bowmen, and forced the invaders to reëmbark, with loss of 200 men and three pirogues, of which he took one.

Saenz was succeeded by Don Miguel Gomez de Lara, in 1681.

The pirates continued marauding the coasts and attacking the settlements whenever they could. They landed in Caldera, attacked and took the City of Esparza, sacked and burned it. The inhabitants fled to Bagaces and the interior. Those who had been taken prisoners were liberated on reaching the vessels. In 1684 the enemy attempted to enter Nicoya, but were driven off, and escaped by swimming. Their small boats were captured and burned by the Spaniards.

In 1718 there was neither barber, surgeon, doctor, nor drug-store. There were no stores. Each inhabitant, including the Governor, had to plant for his own consumption. In the Capital meat was sold but twice a week. The civilized population was united almost exclusively in Cartago and Esparza, the number being few in the latter. Exportation was reduced to some quintals of cocoa and tallow, which were exchanged in Panama for clothes. In 1719 members of the militia could not present themselves for review for lack of proper clothing.

This was the condition of the Province when General Don Diego de la Haya y Fernandez became Governor. He undertook to combat the evils which afflicted it. He sent information to the Court of Spain, and proposed various methods for its defense and betterment. He obtained the rehabilitation of the Port of Caldera for the commerce of coasting-trade with the other provinces of Guatemala and New Spain—although not until two years after having petitioned for it.

From 1703 the then Governor, Don Francisco Bruno Serrano de Reyna, had endeavored to continue the conquest of Talamanca, but up to 1719 he had had no success. De la Haya made similar attempts without favorable results; for a long time he occupied himself with maintaining dominion over Boruca, that being considered indispensable for traffic with Panama. The time of his government is cited as the beginning of a new life for the Province.

ERUPTION OF IRAZU.

An extraordinary occurrence took place in the year 1723, of which de la Haya has left a succinct account. It was the eruption of the Volcano Irazu, then called Reventado.

At 3 in the afternoon of February 16th, there was seen over its summit that which at first was thought to be a cloud, but which soon was recognized as thick smoke which the volcano was throwing up, and which the currents and winds made to travel toward Curridabat and Barba. At 5 there were heard dull sounds and echoes from the volcano, which continued every half-hour, and caused general disquietude. The smoke continued to pour forth, causing a darkness in the vicinity, and giving off a sulphurous odor. This went on until 4 o'clock the next morning, when there was a louder reverberation than any preceding, and a little later there appeared fire from the crater. The thunderous sounds continued less loudly, but were more frequent.

Afterward there appeared at the summit banks of sand, forming a hill, and when this was observed, and stupendous thunderings and noises like reports of fire-arms were heard, there was seen, at 3 in the afternoon, to ascend in the smoke an arc of a yard in diameter and two inches thick, resembling bunches of cotton or snow, so white was it. It continued elevating itself over the smoke, changed its figure to that of a palm, remained suspended for some moments, gave some turns, returned to the original shape, and rose until it disappeared from sight. On the morning of the 19th there was seen another arc like the first, which, without changing its form, ascended and disappeared. In the night there was heard a dull, subterranean sound, like that produced by great bodies of water. The volcano threw out flames, and from moment to moment balls of fire. At 1 o'clock there was a movement more intense than the preceding, and another at 5 in the morning of the 21st. At 10 in the evening of this day, something resembling burning charcoal was thrown up, and afterward it was shrouded with fog. The next morning the city and country awakened covered with ashes.

The same phenomena were repeated with more or less regularity until the 27th.

The 28th there were seen whirlwinds of ashes, which fell upon the city, the volcano meanwhile continuing its movement, although with some intervals of calm.

The alarm caused by the frequent tremblings, the subterranean noises, the fire, the sand and ashes from the volcano, put the inhabitants in such terror that they could only occupy themselves with prayers, masses, and rosaries, and they would not leave the churches when the danger was greatest.

A prophecy had been circulated that the 25th of March there would be a great deluge. Upon this day the people gathered in the churches, terror-stricken, and praying for mercy; but it happened that on this day the volcano was most quiet and harmless.

The quakings did not cease until December of the same year, variations being observed according to the influence of the moon. The houses suffered terribly; the city was almost ruined, and naturally in worse state of poverty than before.

IMPROVEMENT AND REANIMATION, 1727 TO 1821.

The unfortunate condition of Costa Rica began to be somewhat improved, in spite of the struggle to open way for improvements being a hard one; the first thing was to conquer the indifference of the authorities of the Kingdom, afterward to meet the misery and disorganization that swamped the Province. The discords among its few inhabitants, and the questions stirred up with the authorities, had caused evils that could not be repaired in a moment.

Nor had the Mosquito Indians ceased their invasions, for which reason it was necessary to think seriously of the fortification of Matina for the defense of the cocoa haciendas, and to avert the danger of new attempts at invasion.

The decline of Costa Rica was doubtless the cause of the indifference with which she was regarded for long years, since there were no orders given by the Governor of Guatemala in that period to raise her from her prostration.

The laws of de la Haya, as to the improvement and opening of the Port of Caldera, attracted the attention of the Court; but the port referred to was not rehabilitated until 1734, and the Matina coasts continued abandoned for many years. The lack of roads and the poorness of ports was considered the best means of defense against invasion. The only communications, therefore, with the outside world consisted of two very bad roads, one to Nicaragua, the other to Panama.

In 1738 the Governor, Don Francisco Antonio Carrandi y Menan, visited the Valley of Matina for the purpose of studying the best place to construct a fort for defense. He went over the points on the Matina River which he believed most suitable, and fixed upon a site. There existed at the time eighty-nine cocoa haciendas,

IMPROVEMENT AND REANIMATION.

with 137,848 trees producing, and nearly 100,000 of non-producing ages. It was calculated that each tree produced four pounds, which was worth $1, thus making the whole worth something like $130,000. Of this, $700 was paid tax for the priest and $300 for passage and canoeman on the Reventazon River. The laborers were paid $12.50 per month and their food, and the freight of every two sackfuls to Cartago cost $12.50.

It was, then, not a vast business, yet the only one by which the Province lived; and the plantations did not cease increasing, notwithstanding they were exposed to the robbery and depredations of the Mosquitos.

The report of Carrandi y Menan, severe in his judgment of the manners of Costa Rica in his time, attributed many of the evils to vagrancy. There were no schools; the streets of Cartago, the capital, were unpaved and extremely bad; the rivers had no bridges, and the roads were impassable because of their complete neglect.

Although the villages of Cot, Quircot, Tobosi, and Laborio surrounded the capital, and there also were those of Curridabat, Aserri, Barba, and Pacaca, Menan says that they had only 600 Indian population, although but few years previous they numbered 10,000. He also adds that there existed no interior commerce; the inhabitants, even to the Governor, had to harvest the corn for each year, and to provide themselves with necessaries.

Boruca appears the village with most inhabitants; it numbered 1,000 Indians, but it was very far from Cartago, and subject to a Franciscan, who governed it without other authority. It was Menan's province to appoint the head of that village, as also of Atirro and Tucurrique.

To recognize such a state of affairs as improvement is to make patent the grade of misery to which Costa Rica was reduced for many years; but her fertile soil and her natural wealth brought her up in spite of all. Enlargement of the privilege to export was obtained, previously limited to cocoa. In 1743 the fort of San Fernando was built in Matina, half a league from the sea, and a garrison of 100 men established there. The Alcaldia Mayor of Nicoya was suppressed in 1750, and that district incorporated with Costa Rica. A tobacco factory was established, which gave great impulse to the country, particularly proving of importance to the town of San José.

Later on they succeeded in concluding a peaceful agreement with the Mosquitos, who had continued their invasions and caused the death of Governor Francisco Fernandez de la Pastora in 1758.

Although better times were coming for Costa Rica, the change was not really notable until 1797, when Tomas de Acosta began to govern. De Acosta was, perhaps, the most important of all the Governors. His principal interest was in the progress of agriculture, and among other commendable actions, is cited his combating the monopoly of tobacco, whose culture he sought to advance.

Acosta was succeeded by Don Juan de Dios de Ayala, who neglected no plan of his predecessor, but, like him, gave impulse to improvement. It happened that during his government was promulgated the Spanish Constitution of 1812, according to which was established a deputation or assembly in each Province, that for Nicaragua and Costa Rica, in common, to meet in Leon de Nicaragua.

Ayala governed until his death, which occurred suddenly in 1819. He was succeeded provisionally by Don Ramon Jimenez in the political and Don Juan Manuel de Cañas in the military, the latter soon after assuming both commands.

Cañas, because of his health, resigned the government, but his resignation was not accepted until some time after, when the events of September, 1821, had supervened.

The Costaricans, understanding their true interests, felt the necessity of an order of things in harmony with their true aspirations.

In 1812 Nicaragua and Costa Rica clamored against the abuses of Guatemala, and in 1841 the Deputation of Costa Rica undertook to withdraw from the guardianship of that capital.

GOVERNORS OF COSTA RICA UNDER THE SPANISH RULE.

Names of Governors.	From.	Until.
Hernan Sanchez de Badajoz	1540	Nov. 1540.
Diego Gutierrez	1541	Dec. 1544.
Lic. Juan de Cavallon	Jan. 1561	Jan. 1562.
P. Juan de Estrada Ravago	1562	Nov. 1562.
Juan Vazquez de Coronado	Nov. 20, 1562	June, 1564.
Miguel Sanchez de Guido	1564	1565.
Pedro Venegas de los Rios	1566	1568.
Perafau de Rivera	1568	1573.
Antonio Pereira	1569	1572.
Alonso de Anguciana de Gamboa	1574	July, 1576.
Diego de Artieda Cherino	July, 1576	1590.
Lic. Velazquez Ramirez	1590	1591.
Captain Antonio Pereira		
Captain Bartolome de Lences	1591	1595.
Captain Gonzalo de Palma		
Fernando de la Cueva	1595	1599.
Gonzalo Vazquez de Coronado	1600	1604.
Juan de Ocon y Trillo	1605	1610.
Gonzalo Vazquez de Coronado	1612	1615.
Juan de Medrano y Mendoza	1615	
Alonso de Guzman y Casilla	1622	
Fray Juan de Chauz	1628	
Gregorio de Sandoval	1637	
Juan de Chaves	1647	
Juan Fernandez Salinas y Cerda	1651	
Andres Arias Maldonado, Mtre. Cpo	1659	
Rodrigo Arias Maldonado y Velazco	1660	
Juan de Obregon	1663	
Juan Lopez de la Flor	1665	
Juan Francisco Saenz Vazquez	April 26, 1674	1681.
Francisco Antonio de Rivas Contrera	1679	
Miguel Gomez de Lara	July 24, 1681	
Manuel de Bustamante y Vivero	April, 1693	May, 1698.
Francisco Bruno Cerrando de Reyna	May 28, 1698	1704.
Diego de Herrera Campuzano	May 8, 1705	
Lorenzo Antonio de Granda y Balbin	1707	
José Antonio Lacayo de Briones	1713	
Pedro Ruiz de Bustamante		
General Diego de la Haya y Fernandez	Nov. 26, 1718	
Baltazar Francisco de Valderrama	May, 1727	
Antonio Vazquez de la Cuadra	1736	
Francisco Antonio Carrandi y Menan	1738	
Francisco de Olaechea	1739	
Juan Gemmir y Leonard	June 22, 1740	Nov. 5, 1747.
Luis Diez Navarro	Dec. 1747	
Cristobal Ignacio de Soria	Jan. 1750	Mch. 14, 1750.
Francisco Fernandez de la Pastora	1755	
Manuel Soler	1758	
Francisco Xavier Oreamuno	1762	
José Joaquin de Nava	1771	
Juan Fernandez de Bovadilla y Gradi	1773	
José Perie	June, 1778	
Juan Fernandez de Bovadilla y Gradi	Aug. 1780	Jan. 1781.
Juan Florez	April, 1781	

CAUSES OF INDEPENDENCE.

GOVERNORS OF COSTA RICA, ETC.—CONTINUED.

Names of Governors.	From.	Until.
José Perie.		1785 Jan. 7, 1797.
José Antonio Oreamuno		1789
Juan Pinillos		1790
José Vazquez y Tellez		1790 April, 1797.
Tomas de Acosta	April, 1797	1810.
Juan de Dios de Ayala	Oct.	1810 Oct. 4, 1819.
Ramon Jimenez. Juan Manuel de Cañas		1819
Juan Manuel de Cañas		1819 Oct. 1821.

SECOND PERIOD.

CAUSES OF INDEPENDENCE AND HOW IT WAS DECLARED—IMPORTANT EVENTS FROM 1811 TO 1825—CAUSES OF INDEPENDENCE.

With the victory of Yorktown, October 19, 1781, George Washington had insured the independence of the United States, proclaimed July 4, 1776. The admirable North American Constitution was shedding its brilliance like a beacon of liberty which should guide all America; at the same time, France, in the very center of Europe, was seconding the propagation of the principles liberty, equality, fraternity, the foundation of the new era for mankind, signalized by the events of 1789 to 1793.

In the presence of events of such magnitude, Spanish America, where already were germinating the ideas of independence and liberty, prepared itself for the struggle, and put itself in readiness to conquer its autonomy.

Bolivar, San Martin, Sucre, Ricaurte, and other courageous patriots had sealed with great sacrifices the independence of the South; in Mexico, Hidalgo, Morelos, Arazolos, Aldamas, and others had covered themselves with glory. The exploits of so many distinguished warriors, and their victories, were subjects that engrossed all America, and even the entire world.

The Kingdom of Guatemala, self-concentrated, and almost without other communications than those direct from Spain, was so situated that it could not know what was going on around it.

Notwithstanding the efforts of the Spanish authorities to conceal the truth of the victories throughout America, Central Americans prepared for the struggle, inspired by the examples set, and stung by the persecutions and injustice of the existing powers, who at once offered improvements and made promises which they did not keep.

November 5, 1811, in San Salvador, there was a conspiracy formed by the Rev. Don Matias Delgado, Don Manuel José Arce, Padre Don Nicolas Aquilar, Don Juan Manuel Rodriguez, and others, with the object of possessing themselves of 3,000 guns and more than $200,000 deposited in the Royal Treasury, with which to maintain the independence they aspired to proclaim; but their plans not being well organized, their resources insufficient, and the sympathy of the people not yet with them, the plot fell through. A similar attempt was made in Leon, Nicaragua, in December of the same year, without satisfactory results, and the 22d of the same month, in Granada, the people demanded and obtained the resignation of the Spanish employés, who removed to Masaya, intimidated by the resolute attitude of the Granadians. The latter took the fort of San Carlos by surprise, and made prisoners the European chiefs of that stronghold, until, the popular clamor being appeased, the insurrectionists recognized the Gubernative Union, and, as Governor Intendent, Bishop Nicolas Garcia Xerez.

In Guatemala in 1811 and 1813, and in Salvador in 1814, many distinguished patriots were persecuted and indicted for conspiring, or for their energetic efforts in favor of independence. Among them were José Francisco Barrundia, who lived in hiding till 1818; and José Francisco Cordoba, Mateo Antonio Marure, Manuel José Arce, J. Manuel Rodriguez, and others suffered various punishments. Among the latter was the distinguished Costarican, Pablo Alvarado, who was in Guatemala, and who took part in the projects for independence.

The feebleness of the *Teniente-general*, Don Carlos de Urrutia y Montoya, after the hard and absolute government of Don José de Bustamente, who so distinguished himself by his zeal against independence, favored the work which was going on, and in the freedom of the press was found a vast auxiliary for the voice that declared separation from Spain.

In the struggle that succeeded, between the Independents and their adversaries, Dr. Don Pedro Molina, and other prominent men, demonstrated the injustice of the rulers and defended brilliantly the rights of the Americans.

Urrutia, from his advanced age and feebleness, appeared little fitted to maintain the government, and the Provincial Deputation of Guatemala obliged him, in March, 1821, to place Don Gabino Gainza, lately arrived from Spain, in charge as Inspector-general.

The Spanish party included Dr. Don José del Valle, and although this party was large, and Gainza could rely on the governors of the provinces, and on some armed forces, no measures were taken to restrain the progress and success of the other side.

The news received September 13th that Chiapas, then Province of Guatemala, had joined itself to Iguala, of the Independent Mexicans, produced such great excitement that Gainza submitted to the general will, notwithstanding that two days previous he had demanded that the military chiefs renew their oath of allegiance to the King. The Guatemalans flattered him, offering him the command of Central America, free and supreme, and urged him to convoke a general gathering of functionaries, in order that there should be dictated definitive measures as to the great subject which absorbed all thoughts. The idea was accepted, and, by agreement with the Provincial Deputation, the meeting convoked. It took place on the morning of September 15th, and after hearing the opinions of all who wished to express them, Valle said that the desire of those who aspired to autonomy was just, but that the declaration should have been cited in order that it receive the votes of the provinces. The majority was for the immediate proclamation, which was called for with loud outcry by an immense number; and at length Gainza, declaring himself in sympathy, placed the taking of oath in the hands of the Alcalde, and remained in exercise of supreme authority.

The Provincial Deputation and the corporation agreed to the points which are contained in the famous act of that day, an important document, edited by the same Don José del Valle.

EVENTS IN COSTA RICA.

There were those who aspired to complete independence, but, in the absence of all auxiliaries, the idea did not advance. The commerce of the Province was subject to an odious monopoly, and merchandise was sold at exorbitant prices; nor were there any means of ameliorating these and other ills which hindered prosperity, diminished the population, and so reduced it that, though one of the richest regions, Costa Rica was at the time of independence the poorest and least powerful on the continent. As if this state of things were not bad enough, the Captain-general of Guatemala, José de Bustamente y Guerra, prohibited commerce with Panama, the only hope of amelioration that remained.

In consequence of this, on August 14, 1813, Camilo de Mora, Felix de Bonilla, Josef Rafael de Gallegos, Manuel Marchena, José Ana Ximenez, Francisco Castro, Josef de la Ascension Mora, Rafael Taboada, Gregorio Reyes, Josef Salvatierra, Mauricio Salinas de Almengola, Juan José Zamora, Nicolas Carazo, Juan Francisco Franco, Antonio Reyes, and Juan Pablo Ximenez, commercial members of the Section, laid before Bustamente, by means of the governing Political Chief of the Province, a memorial asking that the prohibition be revoked.

Something of the situation can be understood from the following extract taken from the petition:

"It is clear that the only exportation of fruits and provisions of the country's producing is that made to Panama by the Port of Puntarenas, thirty-five or forty leagues of rough road distant from this head city, for which reason, and because of the long distance from port to port, the transportation expense is great, and there are no proportionate results, except the obtaining of cotton cloth in return; by which it is obvious that prohibiting the same to this, the most unhappy division of Guatemala, taking away its only means of subsistence, would be to consign it to the extreme of misery. Coin it has none, nor way to procure it. Its fruits and products are not exquisite, nor appreciated in Nicaragua, where the same kind are abundant. Therefore, with such prohibitions, how shall we promote agriculture, industry, and commerce?"

This petition, with favorable reports upon it by the Nobles Ayuntamientos and the Excise Receiver, was denied by Bustamente, but granted by the King of Spain, to whom an appeal was made.

It must be noted that Costa Rica, notwithstanding the attitude of the other provinces, and her own desire for independence, remained loyal, and even aided in the pacification of Granada.

The Constitution of 1812 being proclaimed, the Spanish Courts commanded that the District of Nicoya be united with Costa Rica for the election of delegates to the same Courts, and for the Provincial Deputation which met in Leon in October, 1813; and, as if to promote the interest of Costa Rica, decreed, in 1814, the rehabilitation of Puntarenas.

The news from Guatemala was awaited with anxiety. At last there was received, with great rejoicing, at 11 o'clock, Saturday, October

13th, tidings of the triumph of the memorable 15th of September, 1821.

The Spanish rule was at an end.

DECLARATION OF INDEPENDENCE IN COSTA RICA.

The news from Guatemala had produced great excitement. In Cartago the majority were enthusiastic for independence, and, it being the capital, it was there that must be conquered the obstacles raised by the Spanish chief and a small party supporting him. In fact, the Governor, Don Juan Manuel de Cañas, gave energetic orders, even prohibiting emancipation to be discussed, and, relying on the soldiery, augmented the quartel force. He was working in concert with the Governor and Bishop of Leon, who lent influence in various ways, in order that Costa Rica should declare herself separated from Guatemala, and that the proclamation of independence that had been declared should be suspended.

Cañas communicated officially to the M. N. and M. L. Ayuntamiento of Cartago the news he had received, and that body met the same day, October 13, 1821, Cañas presiding. It deliberated upon the events, and agreed to second the act of Leon, it being established that at the signing of this the Deputation of Costa Rica was present at the Provincial representation at Leon.

But the M. N. and M. L. Ayuntamiento

DECLARATION OF INDEPENDENCE. 245

giving attention to the attitude of San José, Alajuela, and a great part of Cartago, who had declared themselves for separation from Spain, held another session on the 15th, to which were invited the public functionaries, some of the clergy, and other persons; and, in view of the fact that without knowing the state of opinion of the towns in general no resolution could be adopted on such a momentous subject, it was agreed to declare null and void the Act of the 13th, and TO PUBLISH NO NEWS UNTIL THE CLOUDS OF THE DAY SHOULD BE CLEARED AWAY. This succeeded in inducing all the Ayuntamientos of the Province to send representatives sufficiently authorized, in order that, comparing all opinions, they might agree upon what was considered best.

In consequence, on October 20th, there met in Cartago with the Ayuntamiento of that city those of San José, Heredia, Alajuela, Barba, Escasu, and Ujarraz, and while were gathering those of the rest of the towns, a provisional delegate was appointed to represent them.

On the night of October 28th, new communications were received in Cartago from Guatemala and from Leon, Nicaragua, in view of which, Don José Santos Lombardo and other citizens took possession of the quartel at dawn of the 29th, fearing that Governor Cañas might resist the people, who declared absolute independence of Spain, and celebrated the event with music and firing in the streets. That day the Ayuntamiento, public functionaries, and numerous citizens met; Costa Rica was declared free and independent of all governments, with absolute liberty and exclusive possession of her rights; and that she should remain neutral, and govern herself for herself alone, until events should determine what course she should pursue, remaining by the act separated from Leon, to which she had been subject in ecclesiastic and hacienda matters.

November 12th there was installed the Superior Gubernative Provisional Union, with the following representatives:

For Cartago and Laborio, Don José Santos Lombardo.

For San José, Rev. Dr. Don Juan los Santo Madriz.

For Escasu, Don Nicolas Carrillo.

For Curridabat and Aserri, Don Manuel Alvarado.

For Alajuela, Don Gregorio J. Ramirez.

For Pacaca, Cot, Quircot, and Tobosi, Don Joaquin de Iglesias.

For Ujarraz, Don Rafael F. Osejo.

For Esparta and some Indian villages, Rev. Don Miguel Bonilla.

For Heredia, Don Blas Perez.

Don Pio Murillo for Barba, and Don Nicolas Carazo for Bajaces; who named for President, Carrillo, and for Secretary, Iglesias.

At the first session of this body, the voluntary and formal resignation of Col. Don Juan Manuel de Cañas was accepted, and the Union assumed political and military charge.

The following 1st of December a commission, composed of Deputies Extraordinary for San José, Licenciado Don Rafael Barroeta and Don Juan Mora, and of Deputies Ordinary Lombardo, Madriz, and Iglesias, arranged and presented a project with the title of "Social, Fundamental, Provisional Compact of Costa Rica," and this being discussed and approved provisionally, they proceeded to the election of seven voters and three substitutes, who should form the "Provisional Governing Union," arranged for in the Compact, resulting as follows:

Rev. Dr. Don Juan de los Santos Madriz.
Rev. Don Nereo Fonseca.
Rev. Don Nicolas Carrillo.
Rev. Don Pedro Alvarado (ecclesiastic vicar).
Don José Santos Lombardo.
Don Joaquin de Iglesias.
Don Nicolas Carazo.

SUBSTITUTES.

Don Manuel Peralta.
Don Felix Oreamuno.
Rev. Don Manuel Alvarado.

This Government was presided over by Vicar Alvarado, Iglesias continuing as Secretary.

FIRST CONSTITUTIVE LAW OF COSTA RICA AND ANNEXATION TO MEXICO.

Costa Rica remained tranquil, and gave herself her first law of a provisional character. By this law it was ordered that the Province be in absolute liberty and exclusive possession of her rights, in order to constitute herself a new form of government, and that she should be dependent on or confederated with such State or Province as might seem best to her, under the required system of absolute independence of the Spanish Government or of any other not American. It declared that the Catholic, Apostolic, Roman religion should be that of the land, and although the conditions and spirit of the period excluded other religions, all citizens' rights and privileges were secured for all inhabitants, natives or foreigners with five years' residence, always providing they had sworn absolute separation from Spain.

For the administration, conservation, and prosperity of the Province, there was established a Superior Gubernative Provisional Union, composed of seven voters elected by the people. This Union assumed the superior authority of the Captaincy and Superintendency General, political command, deputation of province and of audience, as to protective affairs, being limited in judicial matters, causing the constitutional judges to administer justice promptly and regularly according to the

Don J. Apolinar Soto, First Vice-President.

Spanish Constitution and laws existing; and for ordinary business, the Union was divided in three sections: The first, charged with military and its branches, composed of three members; the second, with political, composed of two members, and the third, with economy and public policy, composed also of two members.

About this time there was received in Guatemala a communication from General Iturbide, stating that Mexican forces were coming to sustain the independence of these provinces, and suggesting the propriety of annexation to Mexico.

The news was made known to the towns, accompanied by an extensive circular, considering the subject in all its aspects.

Although the majority were in favor of incorporation with the Empire, San Salvador, Guatemala, and other towns disavowed the legitimacy of the project, and resolved to take up arms in defense of the proclamation of absolute independence. Nevertheless the incorporation was regarded as consummated, and the Empire proceeded to dictate administrative measures for all the provinces.

The Compact or Constitutive Law of Costa Rica was subscribed to December 1, 1821, by deputies from all the peoples, and sworn to; the 11th of that month, it was sent forth to the towns; but already, on the 7th, Heredia had seceded, denying its obedience to the Government, and asserting its dependence upon Leon, Nicaragua. On the 18th there was received in Cartago the invitation of Iturbide to join Mexico; the towns decided in favor of it, and nearly all took the oath of independence in conformance with the plan of Iguala and treaties of Cordoba.

Union with Mexico was proclaimed formally in Costa Rica January 10, 1822, when it was declared that, the *pueblos* having decided for incorporation with the Empire of Iturbide, this Province should send a delegate or delegates, which they should designate, and be subject to the Constitution that the Congress of that country should dictate.

Article 1 of the Provisional Compact of Costa Rica was altered; and in virtue of the division of the ancient Kingdom of Guatemala in three general commands, Chiapas, Sacatepequez, and Costa Rica, decreed by the Empire, the last should have its capital in Leon de Nicaragua.

Among the improvements of the Compact in question, was that in which the sections of the Union charged with public business should attend to it in the following order: The first, political; the second, military; and the third, financial.

It was also declared that as soon as Heredia should manifest her acceptance of this law, she should be entitled to the corresponding privileges.

The Fundamental Law being approved January 11th, the electors of the Division proceeded to elect the Superior Gubernative Union, as follows:

President, Licenciado Don Rafael Barroeta.
Vice-President, Don José Maria Peralta.
Secretary, Don Juan Mora.
Don Santiago Bonilla.
Don José R. de Gallegos.
Don Joaquin de Iglesias.
Don José Mercedes Peralta.

SUBSTITUTES.

Don Joaquin Prieto.
Don Pedro Carazo.
Don Juan Antonio Alfaro.

This Government was installed January 13, 1822; its residence was to be three months in each of the principal cities; and four of its members were to be replaced each year, while was being framed the Definitive Constitution.

FIRST CIVIL WAR IN COSTA RICA.

Costa Rica having been declared a part of the Mexican Empire, in February of the same year the Gubernative Union ordered that all the Ayuntamientos and authorities be changed, according as Imperial law determined, and that a delegate to the Assembly be appointed, according to the same, in order that the union with the same Empire should be made effectual. In consequence, March 6, 1822, Rev. José Francisco Peralta was elected delegate proper, and as substitute, José Antonio Alvarado.

Gen. Don Vicente Filisola, sent by the Emperor with the Mexican forces, as promised, arrived in Guatemala June 12th, and received the command from Gainza, who was ordered to Mexico.

Filisola appeared much impressed in favor of these towns, and sought to obtain peaceably the union of Salvador; but not succeeding, and coerced by the orders of his chief, he began war against it.

Despite the troubles and distraction of civil war in the other provinces, Costa Rica remained tranquil, undisturbed, save by the earthquake of Cartago in 1822. This tranquillity lasted until the end of the year, when the division of opinion as to the system of definitive government which should be adopted began to assume an alarming aspect.

It had been believed that union with the Empire of Iturbide would benefit the interests of the country; but, acting with commendable prudence, the Government had declared that it should retain its sovereignty until the Constitution of the Empire should be decreed, and the deputation from Costa Rica heard, establishing the order which they would keep.

The election of the delegate to the Assembly being effected in conformity with the edict of the Empire, in a solemn reunion of the representatives of all the towns, September 2, 1822, there were established the principles, according to which Costa Rica should submit to a system of Representative Constitutional Government, and it was made clear that she would prefer the representation of Guatemala, if, according to the Act of the 15th of September, it succeeded in constituting itself a separate, federative State.

It was also declared as a condition that there be granted to Costa Rica the reforms which she should indicate in her former administration, always keeping the division of the three authorities, Legislative, Executive, and Judicial, according to the plan of Iguala and treaties of Cordoba; that the exercise of the people's sovereignty in elections should be with equity according to the populace, and without the unjust weight of the edict of November, 1821; and finally that, as the principles proposed were only ones that could bring prosperity and progress to the country, they should go into effect.

These conditions were not given attention, and, without hearing the deputation of Costa Rica, the Empire recognized the Captaincy-general of Leon, whose Governor and Captain-general, Rincon, was given authority to elect that of Costa Rica. This without previous indication, and after it had been settled in Mexico that the authorities of Costa Rica should turn to Guatemala in case of such necessity, and not to Nicaragua.

Costa Rica therefore protested that she was not obliged to accept without question all that the Empire should offer, and the great majority elected to disavow the authority of that Government, by which it remained in worse condition than by that of Spain.

It was adduced, and justly, that, separating itself from the mother country, it could have united with the nation which seemed to it the best; but during the colonial period it had not been always subject to Guatemala, nor was its union with the Empire made effective, not only because its conditions had not been considered, but also because of the promises and oaths of Iturbide.

These reasons, justly founded, aroused more and more the enmity to that order of things which, without offering any good, exposed the country to ruin and destruction; at the same time the friends of the Empire exerted themselves in demonstrations to the contrary, thus increasing daily the heat of opinions.

The Imperialists put forth all the news favorable to the Empire; the Republicans meantime represented it as destitute of all greatness or power, being unable even to subdue Salvador, that Filisola was then besieging. It was stated that his soldiers were disarmed and dying of hunger, and remarks were passed on the

FIRST CIVIL WAR IN COSTA RICA. 255

scarcity of provisions, which had obliged him to raise a contribution of $2,800, and to send out $4,000 of paper money.

The Superior Gubernative Union found itself in serious difficulties, and, having received communications from Mexico, believed the end of its government had arrived; it convoked the towns, January 23, 1823, in order that they should elect delegates to whom could be made known the situation, and that they should appoint the Provisional Union commanded by the Empire; and it warned the municipalities that they should swear allegiance to the Emperor within fifteen days.

The municipality of Cartago asked for a postponement of the taking of oath, and adduced weighty reasons for deferring it.

The Gubernative Union, installed the 1st of January, was formed according to election of December 24th preceding, as follows:

President, Don José Santos Lombardo.
Vice-President, Don José Francisco Madriz.
Licenciado, Don Rafael Barroeta.
Don Santiago Bonilla.
Don Matias Sandoval.
Don Francisco Alfaro.
Don Juan Mora, Secretary.

SUBSTITUTES.

Don Francisco Saenz.
Don Juan José Bonilla.
Don Alejandro Escalante.

The following delegates met with the Union February 13th:

For Cartago, Don Rafael Garcia Escalante and Don Francisco Osejo.

For San José, Don José Rafael Gallegos and Don Manuel Alvarado.

For Alajuela, Don Juan Agustin Lara and Don Gregorio J. Ramirez.

For Ujarraz, Don José F. Garcia and Don Juan Madriz.

For Aserri, Don José A. Aguilar.

For Pacaca, Don Gordiano Porras.

Heredia refused to send her delegates, and those villages whose delegates could not arrive in time, because of the long distance, were represented by Don Joaquin de Iglesias and Don Joaquin Carazo.

On the 14th, new but unsuccessful overtures were made to Heredia, to induce her to send her delegates; on the contrary, encouraged by the victories of the Empire, and by the threatenings of the Governor of Leon, Miguel Gonzalez Saravia, bitter enemy of Costa Rica, with whom she maintained constant and intimate relations, she commenced to prepare for war.

In this most grave situation, San José, Alajuela, and the Liberals of Cartago considered how to defend themselves against Saravia, and resolved upon the proclamation of a Republic, claiming the protection of the Colombian Government, to which they preferred to subject themselves.

The Assembly, in four sessions, was occupied with the order and security of the Province, and being convoked for extra session by President Lombardo at 6 in the morning, took under consideration various official reports just received from the Ayuntamientos of San José and Curridabat, announcing gravest occurrences in those parts.

The news from San José was that, between 6 and 7 the night previous, there had been a vast gathering of people, for which reason the Ayuntamiento had called an extra meeting in the town hall, and inquired the motives of the multitude. The answers had come in "vivas" (hurrahs) for the religion, the Government of the Province, and its representatives, and the Ayuntamiento proclaiming the Republic, this being the government they desired, and that which they would support at any cost. This proclamation was made with the greatest enthusiasm, and celebrated with music and firing in the streets.

A similar manifestation had occurred in Curridabat the same night.

While the Assembly was occupying itself with this news, a dispatch arrived from Three Rivers announcing that at 4 in the morning, on the 19th, the people had uprisen, and proclaimed the federation of this Province with the Republic of Colombia, and expressed "detestation" of all tyrannical governments, like that of the Empire.

At this critical moment, the Assembly, taking under consideration the gravity of these occurrences, and seeing that it would not suffice to urge the observance of the prudent and safe measures repeatedly dictated, decreed that, the delegates present not being authorized to act definitely in so serious a matter, the *pueblos* should be convoked by means of representatives, in the proportion fixed by Article 10 of the Provisional Compact, to assemble and decide what steps were best.

This assembly took place March 4, 1823, Don José Maria Peralta presiding, and Don Rafael Francisco Osejo being secretary. It engaged at once to reëstablish the peace and tranquillity of the Province, to procure its reörganization under the same system as formerly; but the difficulties were great, and the interior complications increased through the measures of the Imperialists of Heredia and Cartago, who believed themselves masters of the situation.

While laboring under these difficult circumstances, letters arrived bringing the sorrowful news of the fall of San Salvador, whose plaza had been taken by Filisola the previous February, and that Granada was the site upon which Saravia fixed his regard. This chief, always an enemy of Costa Rica, revived the hopes of those in Heredia and counting upon victory, announced his next march against the Province.

The Assembly agreed to dissolve; first sending a representation to the Emperor, and appointing Don Rafael Francisco Osejo,* Don Manuel Maria Peralta, and Don Hermenegildo Bonilla to take charge of the Government, they remaining in charge under the presidency of Osejo from the 15th to the 29th of the same March.

President Osejo worked hard to dispel the tempest which constantly threatened the complete disorganization of the country, when, on the night of March 29th, in Cartago, Saravia having redoubled his threats and ordered the preparation of the troops, a way was found to end the agonizing situation, by means of armed forces.

At the head of this conspiracy were important persons like Don Joaquin Oreamuno, Don Joaquin Carazo, Don Juan Dengo, and others, who, supported by Heredia, proclaimed the Mexican Empire as the definitive Government for Costa Rica, and thus it was communicated to all the pueblos; but the Republicans, strong in San José and Alajuela, organized and set themselves resolutely to sustain the Republic.

The troops of San José, under the command

---

* Nicaraguan by birth. Author of first geography of Costa Rica.

of Commander Don Gregorio J. Ramirez, took up the march against Cartago on the night of April 4th, and at dawn on the 5th met the enemy on the height of Ochomogo.

"It is uncertain which side began firing: from 5 in the morning there continued shooting at random, amid thick, black smoke, until the combatants could scarcely be seen. Cartago, having neither intrenchments nor war appurtenances, came off victorious, losing only four, while the other side sustained vast losses.

"Through the influence of the Padre Quintarea, who, according to tradition, appeared on the scene of battle, and, holding out a crucifix, implored them in the name of Christianity to cease the carnage, suspension of hostilities was effected.

"Ramirez, protested peace, and asserted his wish to enter the plaza of Cartago with his troops and render the hymn of praise to the God of battles, over peace between brother *pueblos*, and proposed the installation of a temporary government with impartial authorities; Cartago acceded, restoring the arms taken, to that commander, and believed order reëstablished; but Ramirez had hardly got possession of the quartel, when he assumed the character of conqueror, terrifying and causing dismay to all. The credulous citizens, perceiving the fraud, fled; but Ramirez, carrying out his intentions, published a proclamation, guaranteeing the safety of life, person, and property of all general citizens of Cartago, and making the same promises to Ayuntamiento and Alcalde, and threatening that unless they adopted it they would be held as suspects and their property confiscated; these latter appeared to vacillate, and no sooner would they arrive in reach of the despot than he would have them detained, one after another, until he had sufficient prisoners to secure his triumph; then he took them with him to San José, and also all the arms of Cartago, leaving the latter city guarded with a picket of soldiers." So runs the *Exposicion* of the Cartago Municipality of May 17, 1824.

It was at that time that the capital was removed from Cartago to San José.

And so ended the first civil war in Costa Rica.

FIRST CONGRESS OR CONSTITUENT ASSEMBLY.

The battle of Ochomogo was an unnecessary misfortune, all the more to be lamented since, at that very moment, the Mexican Empire had nearly ceased to exist. December 2, 1822, General Santa Ana had proclaimed the republican system in Vera Cruz and Guadalupe Victoria. The revolution took form, and Filisola returned precipitately to Guatemala, where he published a manifesto. He considered the fall of the Empire as doubtful, and did not accede to the petitions that he should convoke a Congress;

on the contrary, he opposed the meeting of the Provincial Delegation, which Don José F. Barrundia urged warmly to deliberate upon a proposal directed to it by the Liberator-generals of Mexico. But while Filisola was vacillating, not knowing which side to choose, the successors of the Liberal forces came upon him with a rush.

On the night of March 29th he called an extra meeting of the Provincial Delegation, acquainted it with the official communication, and then spoke as follows: "I see clearly the terrible state of anarchy existing in Mexico, and to avoid the same for Guatemala I find no other expedient than that contained in the decree which I have the honor to present." This decree was one calling the meeting of a Congress in Guatemala, according to the plan of September 15, 1821.

A short time after, the reformed Congress of Mexico put the seal upon the independence of the Guatemalan provinces, declaring they were free to direct themselves as they pleased.

In Costa Rica they were working hard for the organization of a regular government. Through the intervention of Gen. Don Gregorio José Ramirez, the adherence of Heredia to the existing order was obtained.

The General Assembly decreed the new Political Statute, declaring in Article 1 that the Province of Costa Rica was free and independent, and in exclusive possession of its sovereignty; in Article 2, that it should be dependent on or confederated with only such American potentiality as it should be pleased to join itself to and reducing the number of voters of the Superior Gubernative Union from seven to five, and in Article 16 ordering that the Supreme Government of the Province and political and military authorities should reside in San José as the capital.

The Superior Gubernative Union, under the new law, was inaugurated the 10th of May.

On June 8th the Political Statute was sworn in at San José, as it had already been in the other principal towns.

The election in Costa Rica of September, 1823, for delegates to the National Congress, was that of Rev. Don José Antonio Alvarado, Rev. Don Luciano Alfaro, Rev. Dr. Don Juan de los Santos Madriz, and Don Pablo Alvarado, and for substitute, Don Francisco Alfaro; and according to the constitutive bases of December 17th, meeting was held to elect delegates for the Constituent Congress by decree of May 5, 1824. Its first President was Licenciado Don Agustin Gutierrez Lizaurzabal.

The Congress proceeded to name for Chief of State, Don Juan Mora and for Vice-President, Mariano Montealegre who, being at once installed, took possession of their high posts on the 8th of September, 1824.

Meanwhile, in Guatemala, the National Constituent Assembly decreed the political Constitution of the Republic of Central America, which continued in force until March, 1840.

On January 22, 1825, was decreed the first political Constitution of the State, under which the election of Chief Executive took place, the choice again being Don Juan Mora for President, with Don Rafael Gallegos as Vice-President.

PRESIDENTS OF COSTA RICA FROM 1824.

Presidents.	Date.
Juan Mora	September 8, 1824
	May, 1828
José Rafael de Gallegos	March 9, 1833
	June 27, 1834
	March 4, 1835
	March 20, 1835
Lic. Braulio Carrillo	May 5, 1835
	March 1, 1837
Lic. Manuel Aguilar	April 17, 1837
	December 13, 1837
Lic. Braulio Carrillo	May 27, 1838
	April 8, 1842
Gral. Francisco Morazan	April 12, 1842
José Maria Alfaro	September 27, 1842
	March 5, 1844
Francisco Maria Oreamuno	November 29, 1844
	December 17, 1844
	May 1, 1845
José Maria Alfaro	June 7, 1846
	September 1, 1846
Dr. José Maria Castro	May 8, 1847
	March 20, 1848
	November 16, 1849
Juan Rafael Mora	November 23, 1849
	March 8, 1856
	April, 1858
Dr. José Maria Montealegre	August 14, 1859

PRESIDENTS OF COSTA RICA.

(CONTINUED).

Presidents.	Date.
Licdo. Jesus Jimenez	May 8, 1863
Dr. José Maria Castro	May 8, 1866
Lic. Jesus Jimenez	November 1, 1868
Lic. Bruno Carranza	April 27, 1870
Gral. Tomas Guardia	August 8, 1870
	June 20, 1872
	November 20, 1873
	December 2, 1873
	May 28, 1875
Lic. Aniceto Esquivel	May 8, 1876
Dr. Vicente Herrera	July 30, 1876
Gral. Tomas Guardia	September 17, 1877
	June 10, 1881
	June 17, 1882
Gral. Prospero Fernandez	July 20, 1882
Lic. Bernardo Soto	March 12, 1885
	November 6, 1886

Don Ricardo Jiménez, Secretary of State.

PART III.

HOW TO GO TO COSTA RICA.

If you are living in the United States or Canada, you may choose either of two excellent routes, via New York or via New Orleans. Suppose you are not a good sailor, or for any other reason desire to pass the shortest time possible at sea. You decide on sailing from New Orleans. The *Foxhall* and the *Stroma* sail on alternate Wednesdays. You purchase your ticket of J. L. Phipps & Co., No. 140 Gravier Street, New Orleans. First-class passage is $50 to Port Limon. The trip is made quickly and safely in four or five days. On the other hand, you may prefer to go via New York. The Atlas Steamship Company have their main office at 24 State Street, New York; or you can secure your room at Cook's Agency, at No. 231 Broadway, near the post-office. The fare by this route is $80 to Limon. You may either take a direct steamer, making the trip in about nine days, or you may take one stopping at Jamaica, and affording you opportunity to go ashore and see that beautiful English island, a veritable tropical garden. In this last case it will be about the twelfth or thirteenth day before you see the long iron pier and the splendid tropical verdure of the Costarican shores at Limon. However anxious to proceed on your way you may be, you will feel not a little regret at leaving the steamer—you will have been treated with such perfect courtesy, and especially, if you should be a woman, with such consideration and thoughtful regard for your comfort. The captains and officers of these steamers are indeed gentlemen. In case a storm or thick fog should keep the vessel from landing at night, or early enough in the morning to catch the train for the interior, you need not be in a hurry to go ashore. You may remain twenty-four hours aboard the vessel, as it must stay some little time to load its banana and coffee cargo for New York; or, if you prefer, there is a good hotel not far from the wharf; or, if you land early in the morning, you can take the 8 o'clock train without delay. Your luggage you must have carried to the railway station, passing through the Custom House on its way. You will also be charged a general "entrance tax" of 2 cents per pound on all your trunks or boxes. These formalities complied with, the darkey boys whom you have employed will continue to the depot and deposit your things in the baggage-room. These darkeys are always to be found lounging about the pier waiting for such jobs. They are

Jamaicans, and you must make your bargain with them before they start, or they will ask ridiculous sums. English is very generally spoken in Limon. The train will be waiting at the depot. You buy your ticket and go aboard. At 11 o'clock a breakfast station is reached. This is not a restaurant par excellence, and you must not form a bad impression of the country from it. The proprietor is a curious old Jamaica negro. The charge for the breakfast is $1. Pay it with Costarican paper money, not with a Peruvian sol; this latter is worth 10 to 15 cents more, and the proprietor probably would not give you back anything.

Mid-afternoon you reach Carrillo. There is a good hotel there, where you must stay all night. This will probably be changed in a short time, when the Reventazon branch is completed, and you will doubtless continue on, reaching San José at night-fall. As it now is, you take a room at the hotel, and, having refreshed and rested yourself, go out to engage a horse for the remaining twenty-five miles of the journey. This you can easily secure, at a charge of from $5 to $10. Your luggage you will send by ox-chariot, at proportionate rates. Next morning you should be up at 4, take your coffee and bread and butter, be in the saddle at 5.30 by the latest, and ride off gaily up the mountain road. There is little chance of your making the ride alone—there is always someone going. This ride will show you something of the splendid scenery of the cordilleras. View after view will burst upon your sight like magnificent pictures. At 10 o'clock you will have reached La Palma. You will find a good breakfast waiting you at this mountain inn. This also costs $1, and if you desire wine, a good article may be had. You rest and your horse rests. In an hour you are off again. The rest of the ride is made more quickly, the road being smoother and dryer, and also more generally down-hill. About 2 o'clock you can see the beautiful white city some miles distant. You pass through some pretty little villages, and about half-past 3 your road winds down into the stone-paved streets of the capital.

You are in San José, and you are glad of it, for you are tired and hungry.

You have your choice of hotels. The Gran Hotel, opposite the National Palace, and close to the post-office and park, has all possible comforts. The rates are $2.50 and $3.00 per day. The Hotel Vigne (French), close by, has the same prices. It is not quite so large as the Gran Hotel, but extremely home-like and comfortable. The cuisine is the best in the city. If you are a lady, everything will be done to make you feel at home. The Internacional Hotel is in another neighborhood, nearer the railway station. It has large, airy rooms and good table. The prices are the same, or a little less. These are the three hotels most patronized by Americans. The meal hours are arranged thus: From 6 to 8.30 a. m., coffee and bread and butter is served; from 9 to 11.30 a. m., breakfast; from 4 to 5 and from 6 to 7 p. m., dinner.

WHAT TO WEAR.

For the sea-voyage, after getting below Florida you will require summer clothing. Sailing in the Caribbean, you will find it very warm during the day. For the coast towns of Costa Rica you must dress as you would in July in the North. For the interior towns, I recommend, also, light clothing. Wraps and spring overcoats are good to have for evening wear, but for the day-time you must dress as you would in June at home. Light silks, satins, ginghams, light woolen dresses, and white muslins for ladies and children. Among those things which it were well to bring a good supply of, are shoes, kid gloves, little bonnets and bonnet-frames, silk stockings, and shoe-dressing; also hair mattresses, pillows, mirrors, carpets, or rugs, and lamps.

Bring good silk umbrellas and extra good water-proofs, not too gossamery, for the rainy season.

Bring a riding-habit, if you are a woman. As the best, I recommend one of gray corduroy—trousers, short skirt, and jacket. This will defy rain and mud, and will not be too warm if you do not line the jacket. Riding-boots and good whip, as well as a two-peaked cap, will come useful.

MONEY.

Bring American gold mostly. You will receive 50 per cent. premium on it, and it will be received almost anywhere. Remember, also, that every Peruvian sol you get is worth $1.15 of Costarican paper money.

HOW TO LIVE, AND WHERE.

At first at a hotel, very naturally. Afterward you can suit yourself. You can rent a good house at from $20 to $100 per month, centrally located, in San José. The native servants are faithful, but require continual directing, as a rule. If you have a good servant, bring him or her with you. It will be wise.

The greater part of the houses are of but one story. They are built of adobe and brick, with tile roofs or roofs of galvanized iron, and are painted cream-white, with trimmings of light blue or other pretty colors. The effect is summery and cheerful. In the cities they are built joining each other, like the houses of great Northern cities, and the front wall is close upon the sidewalk. Whatever yard or garden there is must be back and inside of the house, and it is called the *patio*. In the *patio* there is running water and a large sink or stand, as a rule. The water supply is good. If you are going to keep house, bring a tub or two and a couple of wash-boards. A washing-machine and wringer would not be out of place. The native washer-women wash mostly in the rivers, whipping the clothes on large stones, and wearing them out very quickly. The process is death to buttons. The houses have mostly large and airy rooms. Carpets are not much used; linoleum or matting of various kinds is preferred. The *patio* may be kept a lovely garden all the year round. Roses and jasmine bloom eternally. Usually there is an orange or a lemon tree bearing fruit conveniently for the household.

The sidewalks are narrow, and mostly of brick. The streets are drained with narrow gutters, which are kept very clean. There are but few private carriages in the country. In San José there are public hacks, carry-alls, running between the railway station and the principal hotels. For cartage of every description the ox-carts are employed.

You buy all your meats, vegetables, fruits, and kitchen supplies at the markets in San José, Cartago, and other towns. Saturday is the principal "market-day," when all the country people come to town and bring fresh produce of every description. The streets about the market-place then are crowded with oxen and carts and gaily dressed, lively, but always polite and well-behaved, country folk.

The *neveria* (ice-cream and soda-water establishment), near the market, is crowded that day.

Meat is rather dear; vegetables and fruit very cheap. Bread is bought at the various *panaderias* to be found in every neighborhood. The French bread and *pan dulce* are both excellent.

It is a very safe and honest country. There is little theft, and hardly any murders are committed. The houses stand open all day long. Anyone might enter, but no one cares to take what does not belong to him.

Twice every week, Sundays and Thursdays, the military band of San José gives a concert in Central Park at half-past 4 o'clock, and a serenade before the President's palace at 8 in the evening. Everyone promenades at this time to listen to the music. Similar concerts are given in other towns.

Balls, weddings, and concerts of various musical societies occur frequently, and are always pleasant affairs. Charity concerts, fairs, *fêtes*, and the like are liberally patronized.

DON JUAN MORA.

The most worthy citizen, Don Juan Mora y Fernandez, was born in San José, July 12, 1784. He began his public career very young, his first post being ensign in the First Battalion of

Cavalry, organized in San José, by Señor Ayala.

The first political Constitution being issued January 22, 1825, and the first Legislature installed in the following April, Don Juan Mora was elected President. He completed his term, and was reëlected. As a result of his wisdom and prudence in governing, Costa Rica enjoyed eight years of tranquillity and progress, at a time when nearly all the rest of Central America was having storm and sorrow.

The State Assembly and Council, by decree of March 11, 1833, ordered that the portrait of Señor Mora be hung in the hall of Congress, with this inscription: "The Citizen ex-Chief occupies this place for his virtues; others who shall prove themselves as worthy shall occupy like places." And by decree of November 6, 1848, he was declared: "Benemerito (most worthy) of the land, as high in office in Independence, as first Constitutional President, who made great his name, with that of the country, by his continuous disinterested services and by the probity of his character, pure as gold."

He was also Vice-President during the administration of Morazan in 1842, and died in 1854.

DON JOSÉ RAFAEL GALLEGOS.

Señor Gallegos was born October 30, 1784. In 1824 he was elected to the Superior Gubernative Union, and occupied other important posts.

He was elected to succeed Don Juan Mora at the close of the latter's second period of administration.

Because of the disaffection of many persons, resulting from certain laws given under his administration, Señor Gallegos offered his resignation not long after, which was accepted. In 1845 Gallegos was Vice-President, and succeeded Señor Don Francisco Maria Oreamuno. He died August 15, 1851.

Doctor Montufar, in his "Reseña Historica de Centro America," says: "Gallegos was an honorable man, a rich proprietor, and a respectable father of a family; but he was not versed in Cabinet affairs. He engaged in economies, and it was enough for him that the Treasury should contain an abundance of gold. He did not attempt to put this gold to use for the advancement of the country."

DON MANUEL AGUILAR.

Licenciado Don Manuel Aguilar was educated in Leon, Nicaragua. His services as Intendente General, as Senator, as Minister, as Magistrate of the Supreme Court, were characterized by the greatest probity, and gained for him universal esteem. He was elected President in 1837, his message to the Assembly being one of exceeding modesty. His administration was one of benefit to the public good. During it a law was decreed granting rights of citizenship to strangers who married in the country. Many important roads were built, and ports improved.

Disaffection arising, nevertheless, the opposition party succeeded in 1838 in removing both Aguilar and Vice-President Mora, and in proclaiming Don Braulio Carrillo President.

Aguilar, notwithstanding these events, afterward continued to labor for his country in various ways, until his death, June 6, 1846.

DON BRAULIO CARRILLO.

Licenciado Don Braulio Carrillo was born in 1800, in Cartago. He was educated in Leon, Nicaragua, and after traveling in Honduras, Salvador, and Guatemala, he returned to his country in 1830.

He began his public career in the fiscal department of the Supreme Court, whence he was elected, in 1835, to the presidency, to take the place of Gallegos, who had resigned. Among other acts of his first administration was the reducing the number of "feast days." He was succeeded in office by Don Manuel Aguilar. In 1838 he was again elected President, and administered the Government to the benefit of all branches, canceled the foreign debt of Costa Rica, contracted in 1826, framed penal and civil codes, organized courts and tribunals, and gave impulse to agriculture. When General Morazan entered Costa Rica, Carrillo left the country to travel through the Southern Republics. Afterward he fixed his residence in San Miguel, Salvador, where he lived and was working some mines, when, in 1845, he was sought out and killed by a personal enemy, who took advantage of the revolutionary condition of the country to perpetrate his vengeance.

GEN. DON FRANCISCO MORAZAN.

This illustrious Central American was born in the Province of Tegucigalpa, Honduras, in 1792. His father was a Creole of the French Antilles, and his mother belonged to a Honduranian family. His youth was passed at the side of an uncle, a curé of Texiquat. He entered a business career, but soon after was appointed secretary to Herrera, Executive of Honduras. In 1827 he himself was elected President of his native country. When the Federation was dissolved, in 1840, Morazan went to Peru with various friends. He returned to Central America in February, 1842, landed at La Union, and proceeded to organize an expedition against Costa Rica. He landed with his forces in La Caldera, in April, and immediately began his march toward the interior. President Carrillo had a force of 2,000 men ready for defense. Morazan and his men were proceeding toward Alajuela, when, learning of the Government troops' presence near by, Morazan went forward and had an interview with General Villasenor, commander of the same. It resulted satisfactorily, the Costarican troops proclaiming Morazan "Liberator of Costa Rica." By virtue of the capitulation, Carrillo and Bonilla delivered up the command, and Morazan was the object of popular enthusiasm and admiration. On July 10th a meeting of the Constituent Assembly was called by Morazan, and a few days after it declared that Costa Rica again would enter upon the federal regimen, adopting, as far as possible, the Constitution of 1825. After laboring for the benefit and advancement of the country for months, Morazan fell a victim to the treachery and cowardice of supposed friends, on the glorious 15th of September, 1842.

DON JOSÉ MARIA ALFARO.

The laws which had been in force during Morazan's brief administration being annulled, by decree of September 23, 1842, Don José Maria Alfaro was declared provisional executive. Alfaro's administration was marked as a liberal one, also by important decrees providing for the building of new roads and the improvement of the ports, and for the advancement of educational institutions. The fame of this progressive-minded man would have shone more brightly, perhaps, but for his having promoted the laws of Alajuela, of which town he was a citizen, and which brought about his resignation in 1847, and his banishment from the country, with his brother, Don Florentino, and others concerned in the same.

DON FRANCISCO MARIA OREAMUNO.

Señor Oreamuno was born in Cartago, in 1800. He was distinguished for his republican ideas from the beginning of the Independence. His services to Costa Rica were many and important ones—many times in Congress as delegate, charged with the mission to Nicaragua in reference to the boundary question, and elected President in 1844. He was afterward Governor of Cartago, and in 1850 was elected Vice-President, and reëlected to this in 1853, which office he filled during the time of the Walker War in Nicaragua. Costa Rica, obliged to take up arms for her own defense at that time, owed much to the prudence, the probity, and the experience of Señor Oreamuno, who labored constantly for her safety and well-being. While laboring to prevent the spread of the cholera pest, this distinguished man succumbed, a victim to the terrible scourge, on March 5, 1856.

DR. DON JOSE MARIA CASTRO.

Doctor Castro was born in San José, September 1, 1818. He was graduated in 1838 from the University of Leon, Nicaragua, with degree of Doctor of Philosophy and Civil Law. The establishment of the University of San Tomas in San José was largely due to his efforts. He was Vice-President during Alfaro's second administration, and elected President in 1847. The years of Doctor Castro's government were stormy ones, owing to the various uprisings in Alajuela. The continual outbreaks and conspiracies led him to tender his resignation of the presidency to the Assembly, in July, 1848; but, far from it being accepted, the members considered it indispensable that he remain in power. Grave questions were being agitated, and something of a struggle continued between the two great parties into which the country was divided.

In 1858 Doctor Castro was elected President of one of the Halls of the Supreme Court. In 1865 he undertook the delicate mission to Colombia. In 1868, having returned to Costa Rica, he was again elected President. The honorable titles of *Benemerito* (Most Worthy Citizen) and *Fundador* (Establisher) of the Republic, and the rank of General have been conferred upon him. The valuable services of Doctor Castro to his country did not end in 1868, when he was succeeded by Licenciado Jiménez.

DON JUAN RAFAEL MORA.

Señor Mora was born in San José, February 8, 1814. His first appearance in the political arena was when, in 1847, he succeeded Alfaro as Vice-President. He was not a college graduate, but possessed intelligence and ability. While exercising the supreme power during the temporary absence of President Castro, he succeeded in one day, and with but 200 men, in subduing a vast uprising in Alajuela. In November, 1849, he was elected President. It is popularly considered, that of all the administrations up to that time his was the one during which Costa Rica most advanced, and during which the general movement of her affairs was strongest and best. Perhaps no other public man of Costa Rica has attained to such popularity and prestige as Mora. The opposition party, nevertheless, was strong, and in 1859 he was deposed, and Montealegre declared his successor. Mora retired to Salvador, whence, in 1860, he sought to return, heading an expedition against his enemies in Costa Rica and seeking to reëstablish his power. Although his adherents had struggled constantly in his favor since his departure, the effort was unavailing. The Montealegre party triumphed, and Mora met his death, in Puntarenas, September 30, 1860.

DON JOSÉ MARIA MONTEALEGRE.

Señor Montealegre was born March 19, 1815. He was sent to receive his education in England while quite young, where he was graduated with honors, obtaining the degree of Doctor of Medicine. Returning to his native land, he devoted himself to the practice of his profession.

He was elected President (provisional) in 1859, and became actual Executive in May, 1860.

Under his government the internal debt arising from the exigencies of the war of 1856 and 1857 was canceled. His administration was also notable for the authority with which he clothed his Ministers of State, so that it was these, more than he, who formed and maintained political business, and, in short, exercised power much after the manner of parliamentary governments.

DON JESUS JIMÉNEZ.

Señor Jiménez was born June 18, 1823. He was the son of Don Ramon Jiménez and nephew of the illustrious Don José Maria Zamora. He pursued his earlier studies in Cartago, and afterward went to Guatemala, where he took the degree of Licentiate in Medicine. He was twice elected President, in 1863 to succeed Montealegre, and in 1868 to follow Doctor Castro. His government gave great impulse to the advance of education and the betterment of public roads and transportation. The first steps were taken then toward an inter-oceanic railway. He was deposed by a conspiracy formed by Heredia and a part of San José, in

1870. He retired then to private life, and occupied himself in repairing his private fortunes, which had suffered from his devotion to public duties. Sixteen years later the title of *Benemerito* was conferred upon him by the Constitutional Congress, in compliance with the universal demand of the people.

GEN. DON TOMAS GUARDIA.

General Guardia was born in 1832, in the Village of Bagaces. From his earliest youth he evinced a love for the military career. He was one of the first and bravest in battle during the fillibustering invasions of 1856, obtaining during this campaign the rank of captain. In 1857 he was promoted to lieutenant-colonel, and in 1858 to colonel, having received several wounds in action. He was elected President in 1870, and continued in power until 1882. No other administration was so combated with as that of General Guardia; but even his bitterest enemies can not deny his many magnanimous actions. During his administration the railroad to the Atlantic was accomplished. General Guardia displayed humane sentiments, and his patriotism was great. He implanted the principle of the inviolability of human life, and during his administration capital punishment was abolished. He gave Costa Rica a real importance in Central American affairs, and established the equilibrium which there was an attempt to deny. He died July 7, 1882, a victim of a painful disease. His name lives in the greatest enterprises as yet known in the land.

GEN. DON PROSPERO FERNANDEZ.

The administration of General Guardia was succeeded by that of General Fernandez. During the term of the latter, Costa Rica continued to advance and prosper. The credit of the country and its government, both at home and abroad, improved; national products were increased; new ways of communication were opened up, and old ones improved. General Fernandez died, while yet in office, in the spring of 1885, and was succeeded in turn by the Licentiate Don Bernardo Soto, in his quality of First Vice-President.

PRESIDENT SOTO.

The Licentiate Don Bernardo Soto, the present President of Costa Rica, is a gentleman but little over thirty years of age. He was graduated from the University of San José, and completed his education in Europe. Having assumed, and most satisfactorily fulfilled, the duties of President on the death of General Fernandez, in March, 1885, and thence on through the remainder of the latter's term, he was himself elected by popular vote to the Chief Magistracy of the Republic. President Soto is esteemed and respected by all. Under his administration, aided by Cabinet and Congress of men of advanced and liberal thought, Costa Rica finds herself to-day making rapid strides in the march of civilization.

LICENTIATE DON ASCENSION ESQUIVEL.

President Soto, desiring to go abroad for his health and that of his family, on the 1st of May, 1889, called the Second Vice-President, Señor Esquivel, to take his place, as Acting President of Costa Rica. Señor Esquivel is one of the cleverest lawyers in Spanish America, a man of liberal ideas and vast popularity. He was Minister of Foreign Affairs for three years, and is well versed in affairs of State. He was succeeded as Acting President by Don Carlos Duran, the Third Vice-President, to whom President Soto delivered the executive power on November 7, 1889.

Señor Duran at once appointed Don Ricardo Jiménez, the popular young licentiate at law, as Secretary of State. Don Maximo Fernandez is now Judge of Supreme Court; Don Mauro Fernandez, Secretary of Treasury (Hacienda), and Public Instruction; Don Jésus Apolinar Soto, First Vice-President.

SOME FACTS ABOUT THE COSTA RICA RAILWAY.

From ocean to ocean, as direct as possible, allowing for the winding of mountain roads, the journey across Costa Rica covers about 160 miles. Of this distance about sixty miles remain at present untraversed by the railway.

View on the Costa Rica Railway. Bridge between San José and Cartago.

This will very soon be reduced twenty-five miles by the new branch, which should be finished within the present year, and which will complete the connection by rail of Port Limon, on the Atlantic, with San José, ninety-six miles inland, the beautiful and thriving capital of the Republic.

A few years since Limon was a veritable wilderness, having neither houses nor inhabitants. To-day it is a busy, bustling, little tropical town, with one of the best harbors on the coast. It has a splendid pier, built on creosoted piles, which runs out into water twenty-two feet deep at low tide, and the total length of which is 750 feet. The largest steamers come easily alongside this pier. During the year 1888 the number of vessels that arrived and departed was 152, or an average of over a dozen per month.

Direct from this pier begins the Atlantic Division of the Costa Rica Railway. This line runs inland seventy-one miles, the present terminus being at Carrillo, or Rio Sucio, whence on to the capital, twenty-five miles farther, one proceeds on horseback or in ox-cart. At Carrillo there is a good hotel, built picturesquely on the bank of the Rio Sucio, which roars beneath with terrific fury, yellow and foaming constantly from its near volcanic source. The railroad has a large and handsome warehouse, or *bodega*, at this terminus.

On leaving Limon, the road, a narrow gauge, which has just been newly ballasted and relaid with new steel 50-lb. rails, passes at the back of a coral point for about four miles; it then runs along the sea-shore for some eight miles, and presently enters a *puntano*, or swamp, the filling up of which, in order to build the road, was of itself a tremendous work. At the end of this swamp, ten miles farther on, one arrives at the Matina River, where there is a large iron bridge with caisson foundations, having a length in all of 1,439 feet.

From Matina on, the line continues inland, through primeval forests and banana haciendas, until Carrillo, or Rio Sucio, is reached, seventy-one miles from Limon. By this time the road has ascended to 1,400 feet above sea-level, and has crossed the Rivers Moin, Sal si Puedes, Madre de Dios, Cimmarones, Pacuare, Siquirres, Reventazon, Pez, Las Vueltas, Destierro, Dos Novillos, Parismina, Santa Clara, Amarillo, Blanco, Dante, Costa Rica, General Quiros, Dulce, and Rio Sucio, all of which have fine iron bridges with wood superstructure for permanent way.

The new line now nearly completed will start from Reventazon, a point about forty miles from Limon, and will run fifty miles to Cartago, between which city and San José a line thirteen miles in length has been for some time in operation, with three trains daily each way. The

Reventazon line will pass through a very rich country, a splendid sugar-cane region, and one having valuable copper-mines, which, as yet, have not been worked, simply for lack of even a mule-road. It is estimated that 5,000 tons of sugar will pass over the Reventazon line the first year, and double the quantity the second.

Port Limon is only four days from New Orleans, and six or seven from New York. Bananas from this port bring more in New York than those from anywhere else. The fruit is larger and hardier. The coffee exported by Costa Rica during the past season amounted to over $5,000,000 worth; nearly half of this passed out via Limon, although it had to be sent from the Pacific slope and central mountain regions by ox-cart and railway across to the Atlantic. Costa Rica, it may be remarked, is the only Central American country that is able to export its Pacific slope products from an Atlantic port; this because of the railroad. A delicate article like coffee when dried and prepared, for example, will not bear the effect of extreme dampness to which it must unavoidably be exposed when conveyed slowly across the country in ox-carts; and as the freight on coffee to London, for instance, is but $36 via Limon, while via Puntarenas it is $70, there is some inducement for shipping via the north coast.

During the past year 52,000 tons of export

freight were carried over the Atlantic Division, 43,000 tons of which consisted of bananas.

Of the Pacific Division there are as yet but fourteen miles of railroad constructed, from Puntarenas to Esparta. There are good cart-roads from Esparta up to Alajuela. At the latter city begins the Central Division, this part comprising the road running from Alajuela to San José, and from San José to Cartago. There are some remarkable bridges and some notable curves seen on this division. The most beautiful panorama of mountain scenery presents itself to view from the train on leaving San José for Heredia or Alajuela. The stations at both of these places are fine buildings. The station and shops at San José are extensive and handsome. The San José shops and those at Limon are fitted and stocked to the amount of $500,000.

On the Reventazon line, of fifty miles, there will be forty-five large and eighty-eight small bridges. Some of these are very high. The "Birriz" is a viaduct 600 feet long, having four spans of 150 feet each, resting on iron columns, and in some places 200 feet above the water; 3,000 men have been employed; 190,000 cubic yards of soft rock and 130,000 cubic yards of hard rock have been excavated for the line.

The next great undertaking of the railway will be the Northern Road, leading up to the Nicaragua frontier, and touching either the

Minor C. Keith.

Great Lake or the Nicaragua Canal. The branch will start, according to a contract made by the Government a few months since, from Rio Jimenez, a point on the present line between Limon and Carrillo. It will run northwest through a level and splendidly fertile country, of which as yet little is known. It will cross the Sarapiqui and the San Carlos Rivers, touching each at the point where navigation begins, and making connection through each by small steamers with the San Juan River.

The surveys are being made, and work will be pushed rapidly. The completion of the line, which according to contract must be open to traffic by August, 1891, will work a remarkable transformation for the entire country. The road will undoubtedly intercept the greater part of the exports and imports of Nicaragua, and lead them down and out via Port Limon. This because Nicaragua has only Greytown as an Atlantic port, and Greytown harbor is very poor—gradually closing up, according to good authority. In this way Limon will become a port of Nicaragua as well as of Costa Rica.

The concession of the new "undertaking" is made for ninety-nine years, to Mr. Minor C. Keith, the head of the present railway, a man of remarkable talents and energy.

To Mr. Keith and to his able assistant, Mr. C. F. Willis, the Republic of Costa Rica is certainly vastly indebted for their strenuous and unceasing efforts in connection with that which, of all enterprises, is of greatest value and importance to the country—an interoceanic railway.

FINIS.

Arctic Alaska and Siberia;

OR,

EIGHT MONTHS WITH THE ARCTIC WHALEMEN.

BY HERBERT L. ALDRICH,

Who made the cruise with the fleet of 1887. With thirty-four half-tone process illustrations, from photographs taken by the author; and a correct map of the Arctic Whaling Grounds.

"Appeals to a wide circle of readers, and will enchain the attention of the school-boy as well as the scholar."—*Chicago Tribune.*

12mo; 234 Pages, with Handsome Cover Design in Gold and Black.

PRICE, $1.50.

CRUISINGS IN THE CASCADES

A NARRATIVE OF

TRAVEL, EXPLORATION, AMATEUR PHOTOGRAPHY, HUNTING, AND FISHING.

By G. O. SHIELDS ("Coquina").

Author of "Rustlings in the Rockies," "Hunting in the Wild West," "The Battle of the Big Hole," etc.

"It is by all odds the most fascinating book on big game hunting ever published."—*The Journalist.*

"The author's style of writing would make even a dull subject enjoyable. * * * There are enchanting sketches of scenery, pleasing stories of mountain climbing, of hunting and fishing; excellent estimates and delineations of Indian character, drawn from personal contact; a fine description of salmon and their habits, and such accounts of bear, elk, deer, and goat hunting as to make the blood of the hunter tingle in every vein."—*Public Opinion.*

12mo; 300 pages, profusely illustrated; with handsome gold side and back stamp.

Prices: Cloth, $2.00; Half Morocco, $3.00.

Sent postpaid, to any address, on receipt of price, by

RAND, McNALLY & CO., Publishers,
148 to 154 Monroe St., CHICAGO.
323 Broadway, NEW YORK.

Rand, McNally & Co.'s

OVERLAND GUIDE

TO

CALIFORNIA

AND THE

Pacific Coast.

By Jas. W. Steele. Narrative, historical and descriptive. 139 pages. With maps and numerous fine illustrations. Revised and enlarged edition for 1888-9.

An accurate hand-book for the traveler, and a very interesting account of a very interesting country, for the book-case or library table.

Bound in paper covers and printed on finely finished, heavy book paper.

Price, 50 cents. Cloth, $1.00.

RAND, McNALLY & CO.

148 to 154 Monroe Street, CHICAGO.
323 Broadway, NEW YORK.

Wild Fowl Shooting

BY

WILLIAM BRUCE LEFFINGWELL.

CONTAINING

Scientific and Practical Descriptions of

WILD FOWL,

Their Resorts, Habits, and the most successful methods of Hunting them. Treating of DUCKS of every variety, GEESE, SWANS, SNIPE, and QUAIL.

GUNS—Their Selection, how to Load, to Hold, etc.
DECOYS, and their Use.
BLINDS—How and where to Construct them.
BOATS—How to Build and how to Handle Scientifically.
RETRIEVERS—Their Characteristics, how to Select and how to Train them.

The Most Popular Sporting Work in Existence. Indorsed by the Leading Sportsmen and Sporting Journals. No Book on Field Sports has ever been more favorably received.

"There is not a book which could have been written that was needed by sportsmen more than one on wild fowl shooting, and one could not have been written which would have covered the subject, in all points, more thoroughly."—*American Field.*

"This exhaustive work on wild fowl shooting is all that has been claimed for it, and it is undoubtedly the most comprehensive and practical work on the subject that has ever been issued from the American press."—*American Angler.*

"From the first to the last chapter, the book is nothing if not practical"—*Outing, N. Y.*

Beautifully Illustrated with Descriptive Sporting Scenes.

8vo.   400 PAGES.

Price, $2.50 in Cloth, and $3.50 in Half Morocco.

Sent by mail, postpaid, on receipt of price, by

RAND, McNALLY & CO., Publishers,

148 to 154 Monroe Street, CHICAGO.
323 Broadway, NEW YORK.

THE RIALTO SERIES

The books of this series are all works of special merit, and are either copyright productions of American authors, or noteworthy writings of foreign authors.

They are bound in neat and modest paper covers, at 50 cts. each; and most of them also in tasteful cloth bindings, with gold back and side titles, at $1.00 each, postpaid.

The paper series, being entered at the Chicago Post Office, is mailable at one cent a pound.

The Dream (Le Rêve). By E. ZOLA. Illustrated. Paper and cloth.
The Iron Master (Le Maître de Forges). By GEORGES OHNET. Illustrated. Paper and cloth.
The Blackhall Ghosts. By SARAH TYTLER.
The Immortal, or one of the "Forty" (L'Immortel). By A. DAUDET. Illustrated. Paper and cloth.
Marriage and Divorce. By AP RICHARD and others. Paper and cloth.
Daniel Trentworthy; a Tale of the Great Fire. By JOHN McGOVERN. Typogravure Illustrations. Paper and cloth.
The Silence of Dean Maitland. By MAXWELL GREY. Paper and cloth.
Nikanor. By HENRY GREVILLE. Translated by MRS. E. E. CHASE. Typogravure Illustrations. Cloth and paper.
Dr. Rameau. By GEORGES OHNET. Illustrated. Paper and cloth.
The Slaves of Folly. By WM. HORACE BROWN. Cloth and paper.
Merze; The Story of an Actress. By MARAH ELLIS RYAN. Typogravure Illustrations. Cloth and paper.
My Uncle Barbassou. By MARIO UCHARD. Illustrated. Paper and cloth.
Up Terrapin River. By OPIE P. READ. Cloth and paper.
Jacob Valmont, Manager. By GEO. A. WALL and G. B. HECKEL. Illustrated. Cloth and paper.
Herbert Severance. By M. FRENCH-SHELDON.
Kings in Exile. By A. DAUDET. Illustrated. Cloth and paper.
The Abbe Constantin. By LUDOVIC HALEVY, with Thirty-six Illustrations by Madeleine Lemaire. Double number. Half morocco, gilt top, $2.00.
Ned Stafford's Experiences in the United States. By PHILIP MILFORD.
The New Prodigal. By STEPHEN PAUL SHEFFIELD.

LATER LISTS CAN BE HAD ON APPLICATION.

Rand, McNally & Co., Publishers,
148 to 154 Monroe Street, CHICAGO.
323 Broadway, NEW YORK.